O9-ABF-820

The NO-NONSENSE GUIDE to
GLOBAL FINANCE

Peter Stalker

'Publishers have created lists of short books that
discuss the questions that your average [electoral]
candidate will only ever touch if armed with a
slogan and a soundbite. Together [such books] hint
at a resurgence of the grand educational tradition...
Closest to the hot headline issues are *The No-
Nonsense Guides*. These target those topics that a
large army of voters care about, but that politicos
evade. Arguments, figures and documents combine
to prove that good journalism is far too important
to be left to (most) journalists.'

Boyd Tonkin,
The Independent,
London

About the author

Peter Stalker is a writer and editor based in Oxford in the United Kingdom. His most recent books are the *No-Nonsense Guide to International Migration* (New Internationalist, 2008), the *Oxford Guide to Countries of the World* (Oxford University Press, 2007) and the *First Parliament of Asia: A history of the UN Economic and Social Commission for Asia and the Pacific* (Bangkok, ESCAP 2007).

He is a former co-editor of **New Internationalist** magazine and the editor of the initial series of *Human Development Reports* produced in the 1990s in New York by the United Nations Development Programme. He has a special interest in international migration on which he has worked as a consultant to the International Labour Organization, written three books, and maintains the online *Stalker's Guide to International Migration*. This and other sites are available from his website www.pstalker.com.

Although his early experience in development issues was in Latin America, most of his work in developing countries in recent years has been in Asia. In Bangkok, for example, he has worked with the United Nations in assessing the achievement of the Millennium Development Goals across Asia and the Pacific, and in Jakarta he has written a series of national human development reports for Indonesia. He has also worked on numerous reports on economic and social development for other international organizations.

About the New Internationalist

The **New Internationalist** is an independent not-for-profit publishing co-operative. Our mission is to report on issues of global justice. We publish informative current affairs and popular reference titles, complemented by world food, photography and gift books as well as calendars, diaries, maps and posters – all with a global justice world view.

If you like this *No-Nonsense Guide* you'll also enjoy the **New Internationalist** magazine. Each month it takes a different subject such as *Trade Justice*, *Afghanistan* or *Clean Start: building a fairer global economy*, exploring and explaining the issues in a concise way; the magazine is full of photos, charts and graphs as well as music, film and book reviews, country profiles, interviews and news.

To find out more about the **New Internationalist**, visit our website at **www.newint.org**

The **NO-NONSENSE GUIDE** to

GLOBAL FINANCE

Peter Stalker

The No-Nonsense Guide to Global Finance
Published in the UK in 2009 by New Internationalist™ Publications Ltd
55 Rectory Road
Oxford OX4 1BW, UK
www.newint.org
New Internationalist is a registered trade mark.

Cover image: Buying vegetables in the market with Zambian kwacha notes.
Crispin Hughes/Panos

Series editor: Troth Wells and Chris Brazier
Design by New Internationalist Publications Ltd.

 Printed on recycled paper by T J Press International, Cornwall, UK
who hold environmental accreditation ISO 14001.

British Library Cataloguing-in-Publication Data.
A catalogue record for this book is available from the British Library.

Library of Congress Cataloguing-in-Publication Data.
A catalogue for this book is available from the Library of Congress.

ISBN 978-1-906523-18-3

CONTENTS

Foreword

FOR YEARS, THE world of finance had become more and more distant from the ordinary citizen, its dynamics increasingly shrouded by arcane terms such as short-selling, credit default swaps and securitization. With banks pushing credit cards on people, with seeming disregard for their credit history, and offering them mortgages at low interest rates, many were happy to be swept along by the financial flow without really understanding what was going on. When people were advised by bankers that keeping their money in savings accounts was old-fashioned, and they were foregoing tremendous profits by not putting their money in high-interest-bearing accounts that would allow the banks to make money for them, they were all too happy to oblige, accepting their banker's word that there was no way for them to lose.

Now that fantastic world has collapsed, and millions of unsuspecting citizens have been dragged to the brink of personal disaster by forces they could not understand. With private pensions rendered worthless because their banks are saddled by billions of dollars' worth of toxic subprime securities, with houses now worth much less than the value of their mortgages, with the banks jacking up interest rates on their credit cards, people are paying the price of what turned out to be a crazy world of high finance whose dynamics were ill understood even by many of its key operators. It was so unregulated that swindlers like US businessman Bernard Madoff could get away with an elaborate Ponzi scheme (fraudulent investment) for years.

But the story is not over. The collapse of the financial economy is now bringing down the real economy. This runs on credit, and once the banks stop lending because they have to hoard their cash to cover their holdings of toxic subprime securities, the real economy grinds to a halt. Some 650,000 jobs are now being lost monthly in the US. But it is not only the people in the North that are affected. The demand for imports from China and other parts of the developing world has crashed, throwing millions out of work – in the case of China, about 20 million workers in the last few months alone. The financial collapse has brought the world to the brink of a depression.

Had Peter Stalker's concise explanation been available earlier, many people it might have reached may well have been more circumspect in relating to the financial economy. Stalker does an excellent job of deconstructing finance, taking us from the origins of money to the development of banks, on to the world of high finance, and finally to the great crash of 2007-2008. Complex terms such as futures and derivatives are explained simply, though there is a limit to understanding the dynamics of some these instruments. Even the US billionaire investor Warren Buffet admitted he could not understand how derivatives worked, eventually calling them 'financial weapons of mass destruction'.

The author ends this *No-Nonsense Guide* with many reasonable proposals to regulate finance, including taxes on capital movements, tight regulation of hedge funds, banning of certain derivatives and tight regulation of others, the closing down of tax havens, and higher equity-to-loan ratios. This writer would add others. I would abolish the G-20, the Financial Stability Forum, the Basel Process, and the IMF, and support the establishment of a global financial authority under the umbrella of the United Nations. The aim of financial reform must no longer be to allow a few to corner financial profits. It must be, as the author says, to get banking and finance back to its primordial task of connecting savers to the people who need the money.

Walden Bello
waldenbello.org
President of Freedom from Debt Coalition
and Executive Director of Focus on the
Global South Manila, Philippines

Introduction

AT THE END of 2008 an investment banker was discovered to have swindled his clients out of $50 billion. In any other year, this news would have sent shockwaves around global financial markets. After all Nick Leeson, the 'rogue trader' who in 1996 had single-handedly brought down the investment bank Barings had cost his employers $1.4 billion and for this he became a global celebrity, played in a movie by Ewan McGregor no less. But 2008 was not an ordinary year. US investment manager Bernard Madoff had provoked losses greater than the annual output of more than 100 countries yet his exploits were greeted merely with tired resignation and a few jokes about his apposite name. A greedy, incompetent or criminal banker siphoning off $50 billion? Just another financial disaster.

What a turnaround. Until 2007 financiers were the hallowed masters of the universe. In the US, for example, banks in 2006 made more profits than the global retailing, pharmaceutical and automotive sectors combined. Politicians groveled at the financiers' feet, gracing these untouchables with imperceptible regulation that permitted the City of London, for example, to act as an offshore financial center. Even the most nondescript traders, the barrow boys of the securities markets, were able to trouser annual multi-million-dollar bonuses and roar off in their Ferraris.

When the crash came in 2008 it was dramatic. While the details are complex, the ultimate cause was simple. The banks had no idea of whom they were really lending to. Even the employees who had an inkling of the fragility of it all had little incentive to blow any whistles. They were earning more in a month than most of the world's people earn in a lifetime.

We now know that those lavish bonuses derived not from incredible financial acumen but from the more humdrum reality of a deeply hidden state subsidy. Large-scale banking, while ostensibly the archetypal free-booting capitalist enterprise, was in practice underpinned by state guarantees. Banks were well aware that once they were large enough, and intricately enmeshed with other banks, they could be considered too big to fail. So while they could channel their profits and bonuses strictly into private pockets, when disaster struck they knew they could transfer the losses to the public purse.

How did we get into this mess? Why have we been conned for so long – and been saddled with huge bank bail-outs and a global recession that will throw millions of people out of work? As in many other aspects of modern life, it is because we have chosen to pass responsibility to experts. Sickness: that's the doctor's job. Unruly children: let the teachers cope. What to do with our savings: hand them over to the banks. But in the case of banks we were delegating not just the task of storing our money, but of managing our risks.

Life is precarious. The slum dwellers of São Paulo, Nairobi or Mumbai know all about this and try to survive through informal systems of mutual support, based on family or other ties. In principle, banks are supposed to help us do something similar. They can mediate between savers and borrowers, building sufficient trust so that one group can benefit the other. For this purpose they do not need to be dealing in large sums. Take the Grameen Bank in Bangladesh. A few decades ago I interviewed its founder, Mohammad Yunus. He explained how he conceived the idea of lending small amounts of money to groups of women – to buy stock for a village grocery stall, perhaps, or invest in seeds for a vegetable garden. At first glance, this seemed to me like an effective small-scale development project that could be run by any non-governmental organization – an NGO. But if you referred to Grameen as an NGO, Yunus would be annoyed. It was, he insisted, a bank.

Over the years, I must confess, I became slightly bored by Grameen (which in Bangla means 'rural' or 'village'). Whenever I sought examples of human development success stories, Grameen Bank would inevitably appear near the top of the list. Then a counter-reaction set in. Some critics pointed out Grameen's clients did not seem to be escaping from poverty, and that its banking operations might be financially unsustainable. Was it still just an NGO masquerading as a bank? As it turned out, Grameen would prove a more solid bank than many other larger and slicker operations. In an era when multibillion dollar financial enterprises across the world have been collapsing shamefully into the arms of the state, Grameen and many other microfinance institutions have pressed on – as have many other mutually owned financial groups from building societies to credit unions.

What these institutions have retained but many larger ones seem to have jettisoned is a close relationship with their clients. Instead, in the pursuit of profits, most modern banks have done all they can to put as much distance between themselves and their customers as possible. Gone are the days when it was a simple matter to talk to your bank manager. At one point, the new improved system at my own bank, Lloyds TSB in the UK, meant that I was no longer permitted even to telephone my local branch. Instead, in the pursuit of greater profits, banks have resorted to higher levels of technology and launched ever more complex and exotic financial vehicles. As a result, borrowers and lenders have been pushed even further apart. Risk has been distributed in weird and opaque ways and ultimately assumed by no-one.

This orphaned risk has ballooned to gigantic proportions and sprawled far beyond national borders. So extensive are the global tentacles of international finance that a crisis in one country is now almost instantly transmitted to all the others – leaving national governments struggling to take coordinated action – bereft of the necessary international institutions. One body that might have been appropriate, the International Monetary Fund, is now deeply mistrusted in developing countries for its ineptitude and ideological rigidity.

Time to start again, and consider what we really need. While the primary drivers of markets are usually greed and fear, the global financial system is far too critical to rest on such primordial instincts. As the Grameen Bank and other mutual organizations have demonstrated, banking needs to be based on shared risk and shared responsibility – locally, nationally and internationally.

This guide aims to look more closely at the options. You might not consider a book about money or finance a very enticing prospect, but if you have read this far you probably want to know more. I have tried to tell the story as simply as possible, starting from scratch – from the earliest days of barter through to the arcane complexity of 'collateralized debt obligations'. I have used many sources, but am particularly grateful to Satish Mishra of Strategic Asia in Jakarta, who read the first draft of this guide and provided many valuable suggestions. I am however, reluctant to share the credit for any errors, which are entirely of my own making.

Books like this *No-Nonsense Guide to Global Finance* should in principle be easy to read. In practice, they still require a bit of effort. If you do make it to the end I hope you will gain some sense of where we have been going wrong, and why we need to start afresh to build a more stable and equitable system of international finance.

Peter Stalker
Oxford

1 Coining it – the origins of hard cash

Money has flowed through human civilization for millennia, lubricating trade and other forms of exchange and taking on many strange and complex forms – from gold ingots to cowry shells to evanescent bits and bytes whizzing through the electronic ether. And as it moves from person to person, money talks – offering a running commentary on the balance of power between individuals, corporations and the state.

FOR SOMETHING THAT plays such a central part in everyday life, money is remarkably slippery and amorphous. Is it an object, or just a piece of information? You can consider as money the coins in your pocket or the notes in your wallet. But if your total worldly wealth is on your person right now you are unlikely to feel very secure. You hope that the cash you have in your bank account also counts as money, though it may never have taken a physical form – just an electronic entry in some remote computer. Even some of the world's poorest communities are now receiving payments and settling accounts using mobile phones.

Money is what money does. Suppose you are in a taxi, discover that you have no cash and offer to pay with your watch. Is your watch money? If so, then absolutely anything could be money – which would make this a very fat book. Since this *No-Nonsense Guide* is mercifully slim, there must be an escape route, via a snappy definition. There is. One of the standard assertions is: 'Money is anything that is widely used for making payments and accounting for debts and credits'. So yes, money can be anything that will be accepted as payment. If you live in a community that regularly exchanges cattle, then you can use bulls and cows as money. If someone owes you five cows you know where you stand. On the other hand if you are three bullocks behind with your rent, you are in trouble.

Beginning with barter

The simplest starting point for all of this is barter. If you live in a small community and work as a cobbler you could simply exchange the shoes you make for bread from the baker or clothes from the tailor – bartering one item for another. But your fellow artisans might not want shoes right now. Maybe they would prefer potatoes or geese or help with their harvest. Since life is too short to keep track of other people's current needs, or their shoe sizes, a neater solution is for people to pay each other with common items that everyone will accept.

This signals one of the most important functions of money. It is a medium of exchange. For this purpose you could use any readily transferable commodity but the best bet will be something in limited supply. If you could just pick up any old stone from the ground and offered to buy bread with this, the baker would not be very impressed. Throughout the ages the most common forms of 'commodity money' have been precious metals, and particularly silver and gold which have the merit of being relatively scarce and portable while also being divisible into any size and weight.

Precious metals are also durable, which is why even when many other elements of ancient cultures have disappeared, pieces of money often remain as the most persistent vestiges of human activity. The earliest known usages of commodity money have been traced back to the 24th century BC, in Mesopotamia, the land between the Tigris and Euphrates rivers, which is now shared between Iraq, Syria and Turkey. Here people often used both silver and grain when exchanging goods. They could also use these for paying fines. Around 1000 years BC the king of Eshnunna in northern Mesopotamia, for example, declared that the fine for biting a man's nose was around half a kilo of silver.[1] To allow for other lesser offenses, and different trading activities, the metal was cast into ingots, or broken into small scraps, or extruded into a wire that could be clipped to an appropriate length. Another metal with a long history as a means of exchange is copper: in Ancient Egypt for around 4 kilograms you could get an ox.

Of course metals that are scarce in some places can be quite common in others. So if you lived in, or better yet owned, a place that had a gratifying supply of precious metals you would literally be sitting on a goldmine. Lydia, for example, a territory in what is now Turkey, was well endowed with a natural gold-silver alloy called electrum. The last king of Lydia, from 560 BC, was Croesus who became fabulously wealthy; indeed he was 'as rich as Croesus'.

Slotting in coins

Lydia is also thought to have been the first place to introduce coins – casting different weights of gold or silver so as to offer a system of regular oval pieces stamped on either face with different symbols according to the value. Instead of carrying around a pair of scales to tell how much metal you were exchanging you could instead accept the coins at 'face value'.

Coins were also being produced in city states in ancient Greece. In Athens, for example, the government would pay citizens with coins for public service activities, from fighting (as soldiers) to taking turns in juries. At first the face value of the coins matched the value of the metal they contained. But this proved awkward for the smallest transactions which might require tiny scraps of silver, so the Greek cities also started to issue bronze coins, simply asserting their value, which was generally greater than their metal content. This represented an early example of what might be called token or 'fiat' money.[2]

Coining it

Soon Athens was making similar declarations about gold or silver coins, imposing a value higher than the actual metal content. It could do this by ensuring that only the state could produce the coins and making it clear that it would prosecute any forgers. This was also an early example of 'seignorage' – the power over money creation that allows the government to manufacture money and use it to pay its own bills. Athens also saw the first signs of what we now call bankers. These started out as moneychangers, providing foreigners arriving in the city with coins they would need for daily transactions. But some moneychangers also started to store coins, and lend them out – at an interest rate of around 12 per cent per year.

To make the value readily identifiable the coins were originally stamped with symbols such as plants or animals. In Athens, for example, one of the coins carried a stamp of their sacred bird and became known as an 'owl'. Eventually, however, the temptation for rulers to portray themselves on the coinage proved irresistible. The first monarch of this era to decide that coins would look better if adorned with his face was Alexander the Great who by around the third century BC had conquered most of the known world and felt entitled to lord it over its money as well.

When in Rome

A couple of centuries later the Romans too took up the idea of making coins. They also introduced some of our modern terminology. One of the first places they used to manufacture coins was near a temple, located on the Capitol, the citadel of Rome. The goddess occupying that temple was Juno Moneta, from whom are derived the words 'money' and the place where coins are made, the 'mint'. Juno's function as a goddess, appropriately enough for this risky commodity, was the 'one who warns'.

In Rome the basic unit of currency was the bronze

coin, the 'as', which was literally the value of an ass. The principal silver coin was named the denarius which in 212 BC could buy 10 asses. The Romans also gave an early indication of the power of money, or at least the power of money backed by brute force. As they crushed other regimes across Europe they grabbed most of the local precious metals. In 167 BC, when the Romans defeated the kingdom of Macedon, for example, they marched off with a cool 324,000 kilograms of silver, equivalent to 75 million denarii. In this way they cornered most of the available silver and ensured that the denarius would become the major currency in the Western Mediterranean.

Flush with silver, the 'high net worth' individuals of ancient Rome went on a spending spree. In the first century BC, they were splashing out around 25 million denarii a year on luxuries from China, India and Arabia. They also used this money to buy power – either through well organized bribery or simply by hiring an army with which to seize control.

. In Europe nowadays, if you dig up ancient coins the chances are they will be Roman. This is because in the second and third century BC the Romans minted many millions of them. However, since even they could not seize sufficient precious metal to make the coins they steadily reduced the silver content. In the mid-260s in Britain, which the Romans conquered, they replaced the denarius with the 'raidate' which by then was down to just 0.5 per cent silver. This did not prove very popular. Britons and others started to turn their noses up at coins whose value was set by imperial decree and reverted to weighing out precious metal. Indeed, following the collapse of the Roman Empire, most of the barbarian kingdoms wisely stuck to gold.

The seventh century AD saw the emergence of the first Muslim communities – spreading out from Mecca, one of the principal trading cities of Arabia, to establish a caliphate that would eventually extend from what is now Afghanistan right across to Spain. They too started to use coins. The prophet Muhammad himself was generally uneasy about money and is supposed to have said 'money puts my community to the test'. But his victorious followers found it easier to go with the financial flow, and generally absorbed the monetary systems of the countries they conquered, though carefully replacing any Christian crosses with Islamic symbols that varied according to the religious orientation of the ruler, Sunni or Shi'a. Initially they used gold, largely from Africa, but later switched to silver. By the 11th century in Egypt, one dinar, derived from the Latin 'denarius aureus', could pay for a servant for a month, or buy around 100 kilograms of wheat.

China's 'little brothers'

Coins were also appearing on the other side of the world. In China at around the same time, when the kings were trading they initially used various commodities, including grain or cloth or knives or spades. But gradually they too started to adopt types of coin. At first they felt more comfortable if these actually looked like miniature spades or knives. But eventually they found it easier to make metal disks. Distinctively, they punched a square hole in the middle, to make the coins easier to carry in bulk by passing a string through the hole. The Chinese are also fervent believers in the power of luck and some of their coins, particularly during the 10th century, were considered very auspicious and were known as 'little brothers'. Across Asia you can still buy these, and their multiple successors and copies, as amulets or temple souvenirs.

Unlike European rulers, the Chinese royals and nobles resisted the temptation to put their own faces on the coins. Indeed it would not be until 1912 that the first Chinese face appeared – that of Sun Yat-sen, president of the newly formed Republic of China. The ancient Chinese did not rely entirely on coins. They and the Koreans also used other commodities, particularly textiles. Thus they would often calculate the prices of rice, for example, in terms of heavy silk cloth. However for the payment of taxes governments usually insisted on hard cash.

China also originated paper money. But it seemed in no hurry to do so. Having invented paper around 100 AD the Chinese did not produce their first paper money until 1,000 years or so later, during the Song dynasty. This was a matter of convenience. At that point, China was divided up into many regions, each of which used its own currency often in the form of low-value iron coins. Moreover some regions forbade the export of coins. Itinerant merchants found this very awkward, so started to get round the problem by buying goods not with coins, but with 'exchange notes', a kind of IOU which promised to pay the bearer the appropriate amount of cash or gold at a later date in a more convenient place. If the buying merchant who wrote the note had a good reputation then that note, before it expired, was as good as gold.

Later, Chinese rulers latched on to this innovation and started to issue such notes themselves. But they did not put any time limit on them, and offered the more general promise to the bearers that they could exchange the notes at the mint for gold or silver or, if preferred, less tattered notes. By the time of the Mongol Yuan dynasty, from the 13th century, the government permitted only paper money. When the Venetian merchant Marco Polo arrived, he discovered that China, as so often, was some way ahead of the rest of the world.

Pounds to pesos to dollars

London, by contrast, in the first millennium AD was still in the numismatic dark ages. Indeed, even coinage was rare until the eighth century AD when King Offa of Mercia issued the first silver penny. Subsequently some of the Saxon kingdoms started to issue silver coins, known as 'sterlings' of which they could turn out around 240 from a pound weight of silver. Hence the term a pound of sterlings, later abbreviated to a 'pound sterling'. At this point most documents were written in Latin, for which the word for pound is 'libra' which is why the symbol for the pound is a crossed L – which in a more ornate form is £. Eventually, after the Normans conquered England they developed an accounting system that also involved 240 pennies to the pound. This was to last, though with copper pennies, until 1971 when the UK decimalized the coinage, retaining the pound but dividing it instead into 100 pence – popularly, if inelegantly, abbreviated to 'pee'.

Elsewhere in Europe there were the first stirrings of the almighty dollar. One origin was the St Joachim valley in what is now the Czech Republic which had a number of silver mines. The German for valley is *tal* and the coins that were produced there were often called thalers. This suffered many variations in spelling and pronunciation and given the well-known gift for languages among English-speaking peoples the thaler was often mispronounced as the dollar.

Other coins in continental Europe at this time included in Spain the 'peso' which is simply Spanish for 'weight'. However the prosaic peso does have the distinction of having provoked one of the most striking early examples of global inflation. In 1544 the conquistadores who were trampling across South America came across a mountain, which consisted largely of silver ore, in Potosí, in what is now Bolivia. For three or more centuries they excavated this treasure trove, delivering in all more than 62,000 metric tons of silver to Spain.

This was an excellent result for the Spanish, who used this to pay off many of their debts. But it was less beneficial for the toiling Amerindian miners who dug out the ore, largely as slave labor. And it was also a mixed blessing for many other people back in continental Europe since, over the period 1500 to 1600 as the silver flowed across the Atlantic, prices rose fivefold. This was then transmitted to other countries. In England, for example, in the two hundred years or so following the discovery of the Americas, prices rose three and a half times.[3] If the citizens of Europe had not heard about the discovery of the New World in any other way, they would have felt the impact in their pockets.

The peso was also widely used in Britain's American colonies. Here it became known as the Spanish milled thaler or dollar. So when the US designated its own currency in 1792 it also adopted the word dollar. But where did the $ sign come from? Surprisingly, its origins seem to have been lost. One explanation is that it came from the standard abbreviation of the peso, a P, for which the plural was PS. If you just keep the vertical stroke of the P and superimpose the S on it you get the $. Quite so. On the other hand, the dollar sign often has two vertical strokes, prompting another explanation. The Spanish dollar had two vertical lines on the reverse to represent the Pillars of Hercules, and it is said that these lines eventually got transferred to the US dollar. Since no-one is entirely sure where the $ came from, feel free to invent your own explanation.

Finding funny money

Of course not everyone was trading with coins. A favorite observation of Europeans traveling to exotic parts was that these foreigners seemed to be using many odd things for money. Travelers venturing across Africa and the Pacific, for example, often 'discovered' people exchanging a wide variety of objects. One of the most common was salt. In 1520 a Portuguese visitor to what is now Ethiopia found people trading with blocks of salt 'cut out of mountains'. English colonists in North America found the native people in Virginia using clam shells while visitors to parts of India found local people using cowrie shells. Travelers to the Pacific encountered an even more diverse array of possibilities including teeth and, in one of the more arcane options, 'the little feathers near the eye of fowls'.[4]

While these make for curious travelers' tales they probably say more about the perceptions of the colonists than about the places they were visiting. For one thing, many of these places had previously used coins: kings of Ethiopia, for example, following Roman influences had issued coins from the third to the seventh centuries. And India, following Greek patterns, had a long and sophisticated tradition of coinage from the fourth century, which by the sixteenth century had flowered into more than 300 types of *rupya* (Hindi for 'silver coin').

The predilection for spotting curious types of money resulted partly from the limitations of the new arrivals who, puzzled by complex cultures they could not understand, tended to reduce them to their own simple commercial terms. In fact many of the exchanges they observed were concerned not with commerce but with religion, or social customs or hierarchy. These might indeed involve a ritual exchange of cloth or shells but not as a part of a process of barter. One example is the Lele people in what is now the Democratic Republic of Congo who exchanged cloth woven from raffia. For centuries the Lele, under Belgian colonial rule, were all too familiar with the experience of laboring for Belgian francs. But they also had a wide variety of other circumstances in which, for the purposes of forging social ties, the only acceptable payment was cloth – for fees to traditional healers, for example, or fines for adultery, or as gifts to mark rites of passage.

No matter how strange, at this stage money everywhere still generally took a solid form – something you could drop on your foot or hide under the bed. But all that was to change. Money would become a far more mysterious phenomenon, appearing and disappearing at the stroke of a pen – largely because of the invention of banking, which is the focus of the next chapter.

1 Eagleton, C and Williams, J, 2007, *Money: A history*, London, British Museum Press. 2 Cribb, J, 1986, *Money: From cowrie shells to credit cards*, London, British Museum Publications. 3 Galbraith, J, 1975, *Money: Whence It came, where it went*, Boston, Houghton Mifflin Company. 4 Eagleton, C and Williams, J, 2007, *Money: A history*, London, British Museum Press.

2 The money illusion

As people relied more and more on money, they also looked for ways of keeping this precious commodity safe, by storing it in banks. But then something strange happened. The money in bank vaults started to reproduce itself at very rapid rates. Governments have tried to keep a lid on this financial fecundity through the operations of large central banks but have never fully succeeded.

HAVING PONDERED ON the origins of money, it is now time to take a closer look at banks. Banking too has an ancient history regularly punctuated with sorry tales of greed and disaster. The money changers in Rome were some of the earliest practitioners. Mostly, however, they did not lend money but just changed some of the gold or silver coins of foreign traders into the *denarii* that could be used when operating in Rome. Indeed the word 'bank', derives from the benches, called 'bancu', from which these and other proto-bankers plied their trade. You will not be surprised to learn that they soon also needed a term for a bank failure – 'bankrupt' – which corresponds to someone taking a sledgehammer to the aforementioned bench to signal the demise of the enterprise.

Banks lend money charging varying prices for their services through rates of 'interest'. This word derives from Medieval Latin, from 'inter' meaning 'between', and 'esse' to 'be'. The lender was said to 'have an interest' in the transactions for which their money had been borrowed, and interest subsequently came to refer to the level of compensation for being deprived of the funds while someone else used them. The more devout religious people considered this process abhorrent since it involved monetizing time – over which only the deity should have domain. They thus considered charging interest as an attempt to usurp divine power and condemned it as the sin of usury. It should be noted, however, that interest does not just involve considerations of time, but also takes into account the risk that the borrower might never pay back.

Christians became more relaxed about the concept of interest from around the 11th century, not least because they could use borrowed money to finance wars against other religious groups – Muslims primarily, but also Jews or Orthodox Christians, or indeed anyone who rejected the authority of the Pope. This involved a series of crusades, the first of which aimed to retake Jerusalem from its Islamic occupants. From the 13th to the 15th centuries, these punitive expeditions were financed by wealthy enterprises in Venice and Genoa.

Pious though they may have been, these financiers required compensation, so they carefully devised ways of charging that made lending seem less sinful. Eventually the word usury became confined to lending at rates of interest that are excessive, though what constitutes excess is always a matter of judgment. Any users of credit cards today, who are paying Visa or Master-Card annual interest rates of 25 per cent or more, may like to try accusing the card issuers of usury. To this day, Islam forbids charging interest, though Islamic scholars will advise financiers on how to get round this constraint, for a fee.

The making of modern banking

By the 17th century, banking was starting to emerge in something like its modern form. At that time one of the main centers of international trade was Amsterdam. The busy merchants of the city, who had money pouring in from all directions, soon found themselves dealing with a baffling array of coinage. The Dutch Republic alone had at least 14 mints that were turning out coins of all different sizes, shapes and qualities – which were then mingled with all the cash arriving from overseas. In 1606 the Dutch parliament issued a guide for the perplexed – a moneychanger's manual which listed no fewer than 341 silver and 505 gold coins.

This period amply demonstrated that 'bad money drives out good' – a principle articulated in 1558 by the financial agent of Queen Elizabeth I of England, Thomas Gresham, and known thereafter as Gresham's Law. If, for example, you have what you consider an iffy dollar bill you will be tempted to palm it off on someone else as soon as possible, while keeping in your wallet all the other bills you believe to be the genuine article. In the 16th century people had much the same attitude to coins, especially those which looked as though they might have had some of their gold clipped off. The clipped coins naturally circulated the fastest. One of the neatest anti-clipping measures was devised by the ever busy Sir Isaac Newton who, in addition to explaining the laws of motion, and devising the infinitesimal calculus and so much more, also became warden of the Royal Mint in 1696 and suggested milling fine lines into the edges of coins so as to make any clipping more obvious.[1]

Dodgy coins

Coping with all this dubious coinage was at best inconvenient and at worst exposed the merchants and their customers to fraud. To cut through this financial clutter, in 1609 the City of Amsterdam established what we might now call a public bank. This cheerfully allowed people to deposit all their coins, but did so with due skepticism, evaluating their true worth by checking them for weight and quality. After making a deduction for expenses, the bank would then note the real value of the coins and keep them in storage. The depositor could use these verified coins to make payments to another customer by asking the bank to shift them to that person's storage box. The owners of the coins thus had simple 'bank accounts'. This proved such a useful function that similar banks were established in other cities across Europe.

This also opened up opportunities for lending. If one Dutch merchant was short of cash, he or she could negotiate directly with another of the bank's customers for a loan at an agreed rate of interest. The lender could thus instruct the bank to move the coins to the borrower's storage box or, more likely, just transfer ownership by changing a few numbers in their ledgers. Once the transfer had taken place, the lender started to earn interest, but also had to accept the risk that the borrower might default.

The banks soon realized, however, that with so much unused cash in their vaults they too could use it to make loans, with or without the explicit consent of the depositors. Strange though it may seem, by so doing they started to add to the total stock of money. As the Canadian-born economist JK Galbraith memorably put it: 'The process by which banks create money is so simple that the mind is repelled. Where something so important is involved a deeper mystery seems only decent.'

Would you believe it?

Money creation by banks is based on credit – which derives from the Latin *credere*, to 'believe'. Since the bank clearly had in its vaults a large number of coins it only needed to make people believe it still had got them all, or at least enough to cope with any likely withdrawal. When a customer wanted a loan, the bank could, with the stroke of a pen, create a new entry in his or her ledger asserting that the borrower had the required funds. The borrower could then walk up to the counter and withdraw the loan as coins, or transfer it to another of the bank's customers as payment. For this service the bank can charge interest, at a rate which takes into account all the hard work it is doing, the risk that the borrower might default, and of course a little, or a lot, for profit.

Suppose, for example, 20 people have each deposited one hundred pounds of silver in the bank's vaults.

The money illusion

The total amount of money in the bank is thus two thousand pounds of silver. Then the 21st person comes along. He or she wants to borrow one hundred pounds. Certainly, sir or madam, please step this way. We can open an account for you and write into it one hundred pounds of silver. Now 21 people think they have 100 pounds and can spend it. The total amount of money has magically increased to 2,100 pounds of silver.

Of course the borrower need not actually take the loan as silver. Instead the bank could write a very official looking note with lots of elaborate script and multiple stamps and signatures to certify that the borrower has a right to the silver. He or she could put this 'bank note' in their wallet then proudly use it as payment to someone else. This process could go on for some time. But at any stage anyone holding the note could turn up at the bank and exchange the note for silver.

In either case, the amount of money, whether as the bank account of the borrower, or bank notes, or all the physical metal is thus equivalent to 2,100 pounds of silver. To appreciate how this might matter, consider what might happen if these people started bidding in the same auction. With more bidders and more money the chances are that prices would go up – the ultimate evidence that there is more money around. Crudely put, that is the 'quantity theory of money': the more money there is for spending, the higher the prices will go. In fact the total money supply also takes into account the speed with which the stock of money is circulating, but since that tends to be fairly constant, increasing the stock of money will generally increase the money supply. That is not the end of the matter since this new loan can trigger the creation of even more money (see box *How credit creates money*).

Sleight of hand
But back to the bank. You will have noticed a sleight of hand which if not actually dishonest is at best risky. If

How credit creates money

Banks try to lend out as much money as they can, bearing in mind that some of the borrowers can return at any time for their funds. The regulatory authority will declare a minimum that they must keep available for withdrawal, the 'reserve ratio'. If this is 10 per cent then when a new depositor shows up with $100 the bank can lend out $90 of this. Since the depositor and the lender together have funds totaling $190 the stock of money has thus increased by $90. But this is only the beginning of the process. If say the borrower deposits the proceeds of the loan in another bank then that too serves as a deposit on which the second bank can make another loan – 90 per cent of $90 which is $81. This process will then continue in the same fashion through many other deposits so that eventually the total money created from the initial $100 deposit is actually $1,000 – which can be calculated by dividing the initial deposit by the reserve ratio, which expressed as a fraction is 1/10. If the reserve ratio was only 5 per cent the amount of money created based on a $100 deposit would be $2,000.

When the loans are repaid the money supply shrinks in a similar fashion. That is why any changes in interest rates which affect credit and borrowing have such a dramatic impact on the wider economy. A credit crunch will have a striking effect on the money supply.

everyone awkwardly shows up at the bank simultaneously demanding 100 pounds of silver, the bank will be unable to satisfy everyone. Assuming that people trusted the solid respectable bankers of Amsterdam to have judged matters correctly this would never happen. Unfortunately, banks are faced with a persistent temptation to lend more than is prudent. Remember that the bank initially made its money by charging fees for certifying the value of coins – a valuable but laborious exercise and not very profitable. But when it started making loans with other people's money this proved much more lucrative, yielding interest payments that generated gratifying profits.

But there is always that nagging doubt. Once depositors suspect their funds may not be available for withdrawal, they are apt to bang on the doors, asking for their money back – and thus triggering a 'run on the bank'. Regrettably, that was the ultimate fate of the Bank of Amsterdam. Having lent out too much to the

The money illusion

Dutch East India Company and to the City of Amsterdam it was forced to limit withdrawals and in 1819, after two decades of operation, had to be wound up.

Nevertheless, it had helped establish a general model of banking that has survived largely intact. This is partly because it has proved useful for both borrowers and lenders. When Willie Sutton, a notorious bank robber in New York in the 1930s, was asked why he robbed banks, he famously replied: 'Because that's where the money is'. People other than robbers also know that the place to go for money is a bank, from which they can extract cash quite legally by taking a loan.

To disguise the inherent risk, banks have done all they can to appear solid institutions. They have, for example, constructed even their smallest branches to look as imposing as possible – sometimes with stout Greco-Roman porticos that look as though they could withstand several earthquakes. And bank managers, until recently at least, also wore very sober suits, and were considered the epitome of respectability. Even so, behind the physical and human façades the real situation could be much more fragile. Given that banks provided a useful function, governments have generally sought to sustain the myth of bank solidity – while struggling to control them through their central banks.

Central banks

Each country that issues its own currency has a central bank. In the US, for example, this is the Federal Reserve. In Australia it is the Reserve Bank of Australia. There are also central banks for countries that share a currency; in the case of the euro this is the European Central Bank. While you might assume that central banks are government operations, in fact many started out as private companies. The Reserve Bank of India, for example, was established in 1935 as a private company, though it was nationalized at independence in 1949.

The oldest of the central banks is the Bank of England which was founded in 1694 by a Scotsman, William Paterson. At that time the King of England, William III, also known as William of Orange, was in dire need of funds, not least because of his frequent quarrels with France. Paterson came up with a solution. He would sell shares in a new bank, and then promptly lend all the proceeds to the King who could use them to fight the French. Previously all banks had been privately owned. Paterson's Bank of England, however, would be a 'joint stock' company, which would not only raise its initial capital funds by selling shares but would also be a 'limited' company. This meant that if it collapsed its owners would not have to pay debtors out of their own pockets – that is, they had limited liability. Paterson's proposal went down well. The King awarded the Bank of England a Royal Charter and promptly borrowed all the capital.

Bank of England

At the same time the Bank of England was also a commercial operation that could take deposits and make loans. The fact that the King had already walked off with all the bank's subscribed funds was not a problem since it could use his IOU as capital. The King was a decent credit risk and was likely to repay eventually, if only by taxing his citizens. This effectively meant that the shareholders got double value for their investment. First, the King was paying interest on the loans. Second, the same funds were being used as the capital base for other profitable lending through the issue of Bank of England banknotes. A bank needs capital, which amounts to savings of its own, to absorb any losses should borrowers default. King William was much impressed by this wizardry and took further loans requiring the Bank to raise yet more capital.

The new Bank of England maintained a reputation for sound management. It ensured that it always kept

enough coins on hand so that anyone who presented
one of its notes was promptly repaid in silver or gold
coins. But since the bank had government backing,
few people actually tried to redeem their notes. At
that point other English banks were also still issuing
notes, but these were considered less reliable and thus
less acceptable for payment. Soon most of the notes in
circulation were those of the Bank of England. Nevertheless it did occasionally run into problems after
it issued large numbers of notes and at one point was
forced to temporarily suspend the right of bearers to
redeem the notes for gold or silver. To correct this
tendency to overlend, in 1844 a new Bank Charter
established that the bank could only print additional
notes that corresponded to the gold and silver that it
maintained in its vaults – akin to what would later be
called the 'gold standard'.

At that point, in most respects, the Bank of England
remained just one commercial bank among many. In
time, however, it started to take on what we now rec-
ognize to be the functions of a central bank. Not only
did it have a quasi-monopoly on the right to issue paper money, it also became responsible for the national
financial system, and for the control of other banks.

Pulling the monetary levers

In countries such as India, where the state owns many
of the banks that lend funds to the general public, it is
easy enough for the government to dictate to the banks.
However in most developed countries the banks have
largely been independent commercial enterprises so the
central bank has to exert control indirectly. Although
the terminology differs from country to country the
means are more or less common.

The first lever of control is through interest rates.
By setting the 'base' interest rate, the central bank can
steer banks in its preferred direction – to lend more
or to lend less. Interest rates can be thought of as the

charge for renting out money. If you were renting some-one a car you would take into account many factors. What is the risk that the renter might drive off into the sunset and never return? What could I otherwise have done with the car during that time? Will the engine wear out during that period? What are other people charging for that kind of car?

Renting out money involves similar considerations. You have to consider the risk that the borrower might default or disappear. You have to think what else you might have done with the same money – like investing a money-making enterprise. You have to consider the rate of inflation, and thus the likelihood that when you get your money back it will be worth less. And, of course you have to consider what your competitor banks are offering since they might undercut your rates.

Within these constraints banks can charge whatever they like. But they are strongly influenced by the 'bank rate' – in the US the 'discount rate' – which is set by the central bank. This is because commercial banks often have frequent dealings with the central bank. For smooth operations they need a reliable source of ready cash should they be faced with a sudden bout of withdrawals. This can happen, for example, ahead of holiday weekends when people draw out cash for im-mediate expenses. The commercial banks can smooth out some of these daily fluctuations by borrowing from each other, but they also have the option of bor-rowing from the central bank which will declare a rate at which it is prepared to lend. Commercial banks making loans to their customers will generally use the base rate as a starting point, while adding a percentage point or two to cover their expenses, the likelihood of default, and the desired profits.

Interest rates
When it comes to setting interest rates, governments have two main things to worry about. The first is

inflation. The Bank of England, for example, is charged by the British government with the responsibility of keeping inflation below 2 per cent. If the Bank sees inflation creeping up, it may therefore decide to increase interest rates – to reduce the amount of ready money floating around. Raising interest rates will discourage borrowing, or encourage people to repay existing loans, so will reduce economic activity and thus help dampen inflation. If the central bank raises the rate at which it lends to commercial banks this puts pressure on the banks to pass on the costs to their customers by raising the interest rates they themselves are charging.

The other main consideration when setting interest rates is unemployment. Stifling economic activity may have the merit of reducing inflation. This is fine if most working people have jobs. But there is always the risk of overdoing it, of slowing the economy down so much that there is a rise in unemployment. So governments have to strike a balance. Interest rates too low: inflation. Interest rates too high: unemployment.

That may give the impression that it is possible to fine-tune the economy to achieve the optimum balance. If only. In practice, economies respond to changes in interest rates in the same way the proverbial oil tanker responds to a tweak to the tiller. The response time can be very long, up to a year; indeed so long that by the time any interest rate changes take effect the circumstances might have changed so dramatically that the central bankers would have been better steering in the opposite direction. And even if the general course was correct, there is always the risk of undershooting or overshooting. In the UK, the decisions are made by a group of wise persons, the Monetary Policy Committee, which generally changes rates quite slowly, typically by one quarter of one percentage point in either direction. Because these changes are so small, they are generally quoted in smaller units. One percentage point can also be referred to as 100 'basis points' – so in this case the change would be only 25 basis points. Only when faced with the prospect of a sudden and severe economic crisis, as in 2008, have there been large changes in interest rates – down on one occasion by 250 basis points.

Taking loans

Of course banks are not forced to take loans from the central bank. They can instead borrow ready cash from elsewhere, including from each other in what is called the 'interbank' market. Ultimately, the rate at which they do so will be set by market forces – by the amount of spare cash the banks have at the time. The actual rate in London, for example, is called the London Interbank Offer Rate – Libor – which is also used as a reference point for banks elsewhere.

This might seem to cut the central bank out of the picture. But not entirely. The central bank itself also intervenes through what are called 'open-market operations'. If it wants to reduce the amount of cash in the banking system it has the option not only of increasing the base rate but also of hoovering up a lot of the cash by offering government bonds for sale at attractive rates. As will be explained later, a bond is a promise to pay whoever buys it a certain sum of money each year and to return the whole sum after a pre-determined period. Once these government bonds have been sold they can then be traded on the open market. If, on the other hand, the central bank wants to stimulate economic activity because it is worried about rising unemployment and wants to increase the money supply, it does the reverse. It goes back to the bond market, offering to pay whatever it takes to buy back such bonds, thus injecting more cash into the system.

On occasions, however, banks may be so chronically short of money, and nervous that fellow banks might go bust overnight, that they refuse to lend to them at any interest rate. This has been the situation following

The money illusion

the credit crunch from 2007. Banks hit by losses stemming from, among other things, mortgage defaults in the US, became so spooked that they decided to cling to what cash they had, so that interbank credit largely dried up. In these circumstances the central bank can deploy another of its weapons, by acting as a 'lender of last resort'. If a commercial bank is basically solvent – in that it has sufficient deposits and capital, but just does not have enough funds readily available to pay immediate needs – it can call upon the central bank to lend it funds and avoid an unnecessary collapse.

Solvents and liquids

At this stage it is worth mulling over what 'solvent' means. If you have simple financial affairs and have $20,000 in the bank and total outstanding bills of only $10,000, then you are solvent. On the other hand, if you only have $10,000 but owe $20,000 you are in a less happy position. As an individual, you may not worry too much about this, on the grounds that you have a job which keeps enough money flowing in to pay the interest on the loans. But technically if you do not have any other assets you are insolvent. This is more of a problem for companies, including banks, which legally are not allowed to keep trading whilst insolvent. If you are insolvent, then creditors may take you to court to have you declared legally bankrupt.

But being insolvent is not the same as being 'illiquid'. You might think that being illiquid – which sounds equivalent to solid – is a good thing. But for a bank in particular it can be a problem. Return to the situation where you were declared technically insolvent, but then you suddenly remembered that you owned a house worth $100,000. Immediately you realize that you are solvent. Phew! However because you have most of your assets tied up in bricks and mortar and don't have enough ready cash, you are considered illiquid. In the long term you should be OK but in the short term you may need to borrow some money to pay your immediate bills, perhaps using your house as security.

Banks too can frequently be solvent but illiquid. This happens when they 'lend long but borrow short'. They might, for example, lend someone the cash to buy a house and not expect to see all their money back for 20 years. But the deposits they have received from savers on the other hand will usually have been parked for much shorter periods – for example, the monthly pay checks that customers will gradually spend. In addition the banks may borrow short-term funds from other banks or institutions and re-borrow, or 'roll over' the loans every three months. This strategy might work, or it might not. If the bank cannot persuade the other institution to roll over its short-term loans it has a liquidity crisis. While it is still probably solvent, since the loans it made should still count as assets, it has nevertheless become illiquid.

The lender of last resort
In this case it may well need to borrow from the central bank – the lender of last resort. The Bank of England took on this responsibility from around 1825. Recognizing the value of having a central bank for these and other purposes, many other countries followed suit. The Banque de France emerged from 1800 and in 1875 the Bank of Prussia became the Reichsbank. The US equivalent, the Federal Reserve System (the 'Fed'), was created in 1913 following a series of financial panics. The Fed is not just one institution but a system, which includes a central governmental agency in Washington DC, a Board of Governors, and twelve regional Federal Reserve Banks, which perform central banking functions within their own regions. The most important of these is the Federal Reserve Bank of New York which, as well as regulating New York

banks, is responsible for the Fed's open-market operations.

Having a 'lender of last resort' offers a degree of security. The downside is 'moral hazard' – a situation where people protected from the consequences of their actions are tempted to take greater risks. Bankers, knowing that they have a safety net in which to fall may, in the search for higher profits, and personal bonuses, choose to take dangerous bets. But even if the bets turn sour the bank is likely to survive because governments consider bank failures too dangerous, partly because they fear the political fallout from angry small depositors, but also because they know that the banks are usually connected through intricate webs of interbank loans so that the failure of one bank to repay an overnight loan could topple many other dominos.

Another concern about central banks is that their decisions might be subject to political manipulation. A government approaching an election may, for example, be tempted to reduce interest rates and expand the money supply to make people feel suddenly richer, even though soon after the election this could cause inflation. To guard against this type of 'boom and bust' strategy, most central banks in developed countries operate with a degree of independence. This can be achieved partly through long-term directorships.

Although the directors or governors of central banks are political appointees, their term of office will generally extend beyond the life of most governments. In the US, for example, the seven board members of the Fed are appointed for a term of 14 years, with one member's term expiring every other year. Nevertheless the independence of central banks has limits. In practice most governments at times of economic crisis tend to lean on central banks to take politically convenient decisions.

The Bank of England was nationalized in 1947 and until 1997 essentially acted as a part of the government. But from 1997 it was granted operational independence, which meant that it was given the overall task of managing interest rates and the money supply. As noted earlier, it has been charged with keeping inflation at around 2 per cent – but is free to adjust interest rates as it sees fit in order to achieve this. The European Central Bank, which is in charge of monetary policy in those countries using the euro, has a similar target. In the US the Fed on the other hand has two targets. The first is concerned with keeping down inflation, the other with maintaining high levels of employment. This, as also noted earlier, is a trickier task since the two targets often conflict.

Policing the banks

As well as managing interest rates and acting as a lender of last resort, some central banks may also be charged with policing the country's banks, by monitoring their activities to ensure that they behave responsibly – and will not need bailing out. For this purpose they can keep an eye on two important bank indicators: the 'reserve ratio' and the 'capital ratio'. The reserve ratio is concerned with ensuring that the bank remains sufficiently liquid; the capital ratio with ensuring it remains solvent. The reserve ratio in 2008 was around 10 per cent. This means that if a bank has received deposits of say $100 million it can only lend out 90 per cent of this; it has to keep 10 per cent to pay out potential withdrawals which it can hold as cash in its vaults, for example, or as a deposit of its own with the central bank.

The second indicator is the 'capital ratio'. A bank's capital is effectively its own savings. These derive from two main sources. The first is from shareholders who have provided equity capital either when the bank was founded or as a result of subsequent share issues. The second is from retained operating profits. So if a bank started out with $100 million in shareholder funds and over the years accumulated profits of $20 million its total capital would be $120 million. A bank will need to have sufficient capital to ensure that it can survive if any of its loans go bad. The more loans it makes, the more capital it will need as a buffer against insolvency. A regulator might insist on a simple capital ratio of 10 per cent. A bank with $120 million in capital would thus be able to make loans of up to $1,200 million. By 2008, simple capital ratios were alarmingly low, around 7 per cent. In fact capital ratios follow slightly more complex formulae so that the required ratios depend on the nature of the loans, ie the ratios that banks have to follow are 'risk weighted' (see box *Basel sets the capital rules*).[2]

If banks make a series of losses because of bad loans, they will need to either get more capital or to reduce their lending. One way to get more capital is to issue more shares. Initially this means approaching existing shareholders for additional funds by offering them shares at a discount – a 'rights issue'. Then the bank can try to sell more shares to other institutions. In either case it may find this difficult since the need to raise more capital can be interpreted as a signal that the bank is in trouble.

Countries differ in the way they apply such rules. In the US, banks are policed not just by the Fed, but by the Office of the Comptroller of Currency within the Treasury Department which is charged, among other things with preventing money laundering and the financing of terrorism. In the UK, the Bank of England used to have some of this responsibility, but the situation changed in 1986 with the creation of a new regulatory body, the Financial Services Authority (FSA). While this division of responsibility makes some sense it can also allow banks to slip between the cracks. The most dramatic indication of lacunae

Basel sets the capital rules

The Bank for International Settlements (BIS) is the world's most exclusive bank since its only customers are national central banks. It was originally founded in 1930 in Basel in Switzerland, partly at least because of its location: in those days central bankers traveled by train and Basel had good connections with the rest of Europe.

The BIS hosts meetings and publishes different kinds of research. But it also acts as a superbanker, a place where central banks can deposit some of their reserves. It can also act as a lender of last resort when even the national lenders of last resort get into trouble. The BIS can organize a global whip-round from other central banks, which it has done on behalf of Mexico, for example, and Brazil.

Another important BIS function is that it sets global banking standards, such as indicating how much capital banks should be required to maintain so as to offset losses from bad loans. In 1988 it introduced a simple measure 'Basel I' which divided capital into two tiers. Tier 1 consists of funds that have been contributed by stockholders, plus retained profits. Tier 2 adds some other types of capital which may not exist as ready cash — such as the increase in value of the bank's buildings since they were originally purchased.

The amounts of capital can then be compared with the banks' 'assets'. In accounting terms, a loan you have made to another party is referred to as an asset, while any funds you have borrowed are classified as liabilities. However the Basel accords also took into account just how risky those loans were. Loans to governments, for example, were considered to have no risk of default so were given a risk weighting of zero, while those to most companies had a weighting of 100. According to Basel I, banks had to hold capital equivalent to at least 8 per cent of their risk-weighted assets.

A new agreement, Basel II, has tried to make a more sophisticated judgment of risk. This reduces the capital requirements for those banks taking lower risks. In this case the capital required is only 4 per cent of Tier 1 assets. However, the new system also requires banks to take account of the shifting value of their assets. Moreover, the actual weighting of the risk is based on the banks' own assessments, or on those of credit rating agencies – which are likely to be optimistic and perhaps offer the banks too much license to misbehave.

in this approach came with the crisis in the British bank Northern Rock. The FSA, while admitting that it had taken its eye off the ball, also laid some blame on the Bank of England for not acting fast enough to lend Northern Rock the money that could have helped it avoid the crisis. At any rate, after much dithering,

The money illusion

in 2008, Northern Rock was taken into public ownership – the first of what was to be a series of bank nationalizations.

From coins to illusions

Money has thus moved far beyond hard cash to take on many much less tangible forms – some of them useful, others illusionary and capable of disappearing without even offering a puff of smoke. Banks too come in many different varieties. They include commercial banks, building societies, credit unions, investment banks, and many more, some of which are described in the next chapter.

1 Cooper, G, *The Origin of Financial Crises: Central banks, credit bubbles, and the efficient market fallacy* (Petersfield, Harriman House, 2008).
2 Benink, H and G, Kaufman,'Turmoil reveals the inadequacy of Basel II', in *The Financial Times*, 27 February 2008.

3 Banks of every shape and size

From modest beginnings as the enterprises of Greek or Roman moneylenders perched on their benches, banks have adopted many different guises. Some, like credit unions or microcredit institutions, have maintained strong and transparent links between lenders and borrowers. Others are very different beasts, such as the investment banks or shady offshore operations in tax havens that try to keep everyone in the dark.

THE TERM 'BANK' confusingly covers many varieties of institution, which can have very different functions. This chapter describes some of the principal types. If you are in a hurry, and are familiar with basic banking, you might be able to skip this chapter. Or maybe it is worth checking again who does what.

Commercial banks

The best-known banks are the commercial, sometimes called retail or high street, banks which enable individual customers or businesses to establish current or savings accounts, or take out personal loans or mortgages. While commercial banks provide many types of service, they make most of their money by charging borrowers a higher rate of interest than they give to their depositors.

Compared with the UK, where the banking market has been dominated by just five banks, the situation in the US is more diverse. As well as major international banks such as the Bank of America, with over 5,000 branches, there are a large number of regional and local banks – though after two decades of mergers by the end of 2007 the number had halved to 8,615.

Banks have also been steadily merging in most other countries. In Australia, for example, the big four banks have 90 per cent of the market: National Australia Bank, Commonwealth Bank of Australia, Australia and New Zealand Banking Group and

Banks of every shape and size

Westpac Banking Corp. In Canada, the corresponding group is the big six, though here there is a clear leader since the Royal Bank of Canada alone has one-quarter of the market.

A similar pattern is evident in developing countries, particularly in recent years when banks have been privatized. In Brazil, for example, many state banks have been privatized and merged, and the top 10 banks – many of them foreign-owned – are responsible for 80 per cent of loans.[1] Nigeria has also seen a series of mergers, largely because the central bank raised the minimum capital requirements, obliging many banks to join forces; as a result between 2005 and 2008 the

Big banks

The first table lists the world's largest banks, as they stood in 2007, by their most significant form of capital, which is that provided by their shareholders. Until the recent collapse, the banking industry had expanded rapidly. Between 1998 and 2007, the world's top one thousand banks more than doubled their total assets – largely loans – to $74 trillion, and increased their annual profits to $786 billion. In

World's largest banks, 2006/7

Bank	Country	Capital $ billion
1. Bank of America Corp	US	91
2. Citigroup	US	91
3. HSBC Holdings	UK	88
4. Credit Agricole Group	France	85
5. JP Morgan Chase & Co	US	81
6. Mitsubishi UFJ Financial Group	Japan	69
7. ICBC	China	59
8. Royal Bank of Scotland	UK	59
9. Bank of China	China	53
10. Santander	Spain	47
11. BNP Paribas	France	45
12. Barclays Bank	UK	45
13. HBOS	UK	44
14. China Construction Bank Corp.	China	42
15. Mizuho Financial Group	Japan	42

Note: Capital refers to 'Tier 1' capital, largely provided by shareholders
Source: IFSL, 2008

number of licensed banks fell from 85 to 24. The largest is the Nigerian-owned Intercontinental which also has branches in London.[2]

Building societies

In the UK and Australia the number of commercial banks was swollen by the conversion of building societies. Building societies were first formed in the UK in the 19th century when groups of people came together to save funds to help each other buy houses. The original idea was that each society would be wound up when the last member had secured the keys to their house. Eventually, however, many societies became

2008, however, as a result of the sub-prime crisis, profits are likely to have been less than half of this. This table also shows the importance of the UK, where deposits at the end of 2005 were $4.6 trillion, just behind the US with around $5.1 trillion. More than half the banks operating in the UK were foreign owned.* In 2008, the UK had 338 licensed banks entitled to take deposits. The top ten domestic UK banks are listed in the second table (*Top ten British banks or building societies*). The UK also has many branches of foreign banks such as the Bank of Cyprus that cater to ethnic or immigrant communities.

* IFSL, 2008. Banking 2008. London, International Financial Services. www.ifsl.org.uk

Top ten British banks or building societies, ranked by worldwide assets at end-2007

Bank	Assets £ billions
Royal Bank of Scotland	1,901
Barclays	1,227
HBOS	667
HSBC Bank	622
Lloyds TSB	353
Nationwide	179
Standard Chartered	165
Northern Rock	109
Alliance & Leicester	79
Bradford & Bingley	52
Total assets	**6,263**

Source: EIU, 2008

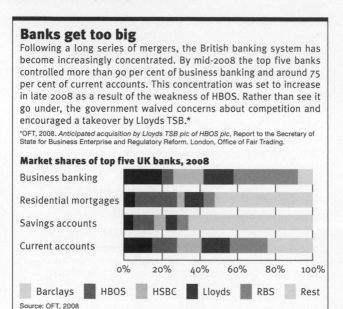

Banks get too big

Following a long series of mergers, the British banking system has become increasingly concentrated. By mid-2008 the top five banks controlled more than 90 per cent of business banking and around 75 per cent of current accounts. This concentration was set to increase in late 2008 as a result of the weakness of HBOS. Rather than see it go under, the government waived concerns about competition and encouraged a takeover by Lloyds TSB.*

*OFT, 2008. *Anticipated acquisition by Lloyds TSB plc of HBOS plc*, Report to the Secretary of State for Business Enterprise and Regulatory Reform. London, Office of Fair Trading.

Market shares of top five UK banks, 2008

Business banking

Residential mortgages

Savings accounts

Current accounts

0%   20%   40%   60%   80%   100%

Barclays   HBOS   HSBC   Lloyds   RBS   Rest

Source: OFT, 2008

permanent, with a rolling membership, and by 1900 the UK had 60,000 building societies – at least one in almost every town. Subsequently there has been dramatic consolidation: by 2008 there were only 59 and the numbers continue to dwindle. In Australia too, building societies first expanded rapidly and later consolidated.

Building societies differ from most commercial banks in that they are 'mutual' bodies. The depositors own the society and have rights similar to those of shareholders in a company. Building societies accept deposits on which they pay interest, and lend money for the purchase of a property which the borrower uses as security. This is the most typical form of 'mortgage', which derives from the French for 'dead pledge' – which sounds rather morbid but only means that the pledge dies when the mortgage is paid off. Although building societies specialized in mortgage lending, eventually they were able to offer many other kinds of banking services. Compared with banks, they are more restricted in the ways they can raise funds since they must get at least half from their depositors. In the UK they can also borrow funds from other banks or institutions in the 'money markets' but are forbidden by law from getting more than 50 per cent of their funds in this way.

Unfortunately, many building societies have now been converted to banks. In the UK in 1986 the Thatcher government, reflecting its privatizing zeal, passed the Building Societies Act which allowed the societies to 'demutualize' – to convert to limited companies or be taken over by a bank, if 75 per cent of their members voted in favor. This proved too tempting for many members who stood to gain thousands of pounds in cash or shares. Indeed many 'carpetbaggers' rushed to join societies to push for such votes and grab the windfalls. In 1997, the ill-fated Northern Rock distributed to each of its members around £2,250 worth of shares. It was not alone. In the same year five building societies and one insurance company provided former members with windfall gains of around £35 billion.[3]

In practice demutualization proved disastrous. Almost all the demutualized societies in the UK overreached themselves, and any former members who retained the shares they had been allocated would have subsequently made dramatic losses. Those holding Bradford & Bingley shares from the demutualization in 2000 would have seen their value collapse by around three-quarters.

Many of the Australian building societies also disappeared in this way. One of the first to succumb was the NSW Building Society which in 1985 became Advance Bank Australia. Between 1985 and 2007, the number of building societies in Australia dropped from 66 to 14.[4]

Banks of every shape and size

Savings and loan associations

In the United States the equivalents of building societies are savings and loan associations (S&Ls), also called 'thrifts'. Modeled on their British counterparts, they too date back to the 19th century. For decades these were regarded as safe institutions, with deposits guaranteed by the government. At their height, following World War Two, the thrifts were responsible for more than one third of mortgages. At that point they were highly regulated; their deposit rates were fixed and they were confined to a limited range of mortgage-related activities.

But in the early 1990s the thrifts too were laid low by inept deregulation, which removed many of the previous restrictions but did not apply corresponding supervision. As a result, many thrifts – some of whom were seized by fraudsters – started to gamble with high-risk loans and by the end of the 1980s many were going bust. In 1989 the US government had to take over and close or reorganize 747 of them with a total cost to the taxpayer later estimated at around $147 billion.

By 2008 there were 818 remaining thrift institutions with assets of $1.2 trillion and 469 thrift holding companies with US assets of about $8.1 trillion.[5] Although now more closely watched, the thrifts are still vulnerable. In September 2008, in easily the US's biggest bank failure, the largest thrift – Washington Mutual – with some $307 billion in assets, collapsed and was bought by the bank JPMorgan Chase for only $1.2 billion.[6]

Credit unions

Credit unions are similar to building societies in that they are forms of mutual saving. These are non-profit organizations owned and controlled by their members, on a one-person one-vote basis, and have often been established in places too poor or remote to have their own banking services. The worldwide credit union movement began in Germany in the 1840s. Unlike building societies, they appear to be expanding. Globally, between 1998 and 2007 the number of credit unions rose from 37,623 to 49,134. In total, they had 177 million members who had $987 billion in savings and $847 billion in loans.[7] The graphic *Global credit unions* gives an indication of the strength of credit unions.

Credit unions have the advantage for their members of giving more attractive lending and borrowing rates. And in some communities they offer people's first experience of democratic control, and can promote development by ensuring that funds circulate locally. Credit unions are strongest in North America and the Caribbean, where the 'penetration'– the proportion of the population of working age who are members – is above 40 per cent. In Canada, the credit unions, with around 11 million 'member-customers' and a penetration rate of 47 per cent provide stiff competition to commercial banks. The first credit union was created

Global credit unions

Between 1998 and 2007 the number of credit unions globally rose from 37,623 to 49,134. In total, they had 177 million members who had $988 billion in savings and $848 billion in loans.

Credit unions worldwide

Region	Countries	Unions	Members '000s	Penetration	Savings $ billion	Loans $ billion
Africa	23	11,849	15,123	8%	3	4
Asia	16	20,199	33,119	3%	78	60
Caribbean	18	317	1,868	41%	3	2
Europe	11	2,671	8,244	4%	25	15
Latin America	16	2,504	15,141	5%	20	20
North America	2	9,328	99,371	44%	827	716
Oceania	6	295	3,915	18%	31	29
World	**96**	**49,134**	**177,384**	**8%**	**988**	**848**

Notes: World total includes small numbers in Central Asia and the Middle East. Penetration is the membership as a proportion of the population of working age.

Source: WOCCU, 2007

in 1900 in Levis, Quebec, when 80 people banded together as a *caisse populaire*. Between 1997 and 2007, as a result of mergers, the number of credit unions in Canada declined by around one-third,[8] but this still left more than one thousand. The largest, the Desjardins Group, is Canada's sixth largest financial institution with assets over $100 billion, 6 million members and 2,800 branches or ATM stations. Credit unions are similarly strong in the United States, where there are 88 million members.

Credit unions have a lower profile in the UK. Penetration is only 1.5 per cent. In 2006 there were 557, with around half a million members and £500 million in assets. Typically they are strongest in Scotland, the largest being the Scotwest with around half a million members.

Local Exchange Trading Systems

Another type of financial institution, though not a bank, and more common in developed countries, is a Local Exchange Trading System (LETS). This involves the creation of a new, but strictly local, currency. The idea originated in Canada in the 1980s and now exists in multiple variants across the world. Although there are no full estimates of the number of groups, the LETS-linkup website has registered 1,076 groups in 22 countries.

A LETS system is essentially a club through which people buy or sell goods and services but without using dollars or pounds or any conventional form of money – quite handy if you do not have much. Instead, the club keeps a central register of transactions. You might, for example, offer to mow your neighbor's grass in which case he or she will declare to the register that you should be credited with a certain number of units, which you could then spend on vegetables from another neighbor's allotment. The units can have any name but usually have some local connection: in Reading in the UK, for example, they are known as 'readies'.

Although some businesses will accept LETS currencies, most transactions are for personal arrangements, hobbies or pastimes. The great strength of LETS schemes is that they promote community organization – and also remind their members of the nature of money. In fact, LETS systems make new money just as banks do, by creating credits in people's accounts. When those credits are canceled out the money disappears again.

Investment banks

Investment banks, sometimes termed 'merchant banks', are very different from commercial or high street banks. The original investment bankers were often merchants who in the course of buying or selling would lend money to suppliers or customers. Nowadays investment banks provide a wide range of often rather obscure services to large corporations, governments and other financial institutions. Globally around half their fee income comes from advising companies that are engaged in mergers and acquisitions. Much of the rest comes from fees for helping companies wishing to issue shares, advising them on what the price should be and guaranteeing or 'underwriting' the issue by volunteering to buy any shares that are not taken up.

Investment banks also have their own capital, initially provided by shareholders, which they can use to trade on their own account. This is more hazardous than managing other people's money. One of the oldest British investment banks, Barings, was ultimately ruined in 1996 by one of its traders (the aforementioned Nick Leeson) effectively gambling with its capital, and losing heavily.

Although investment banks and commercial banks have different functions, they have often had a close relationship. Indeed many institutions are now 'universal' banks that cover both functions. This is risky since a failure in the investment banking arm could also threaten the commercial bank. So dangerous was this prospect that in 1933 the US passed the Glass-Steagall Act which prevented commercial banks from owning investment banks. As a result, many banks which had started out as investment banks and then developed retail services had to split the two functions. After the act was repealed in 1999, Citigroup, for example, and JPMorgan Chase moved back into investment banking.

Banks of every shape and size

Investment banks when acting as underwriters acquire valuable information about lucrative deals; this offers considerable scope for unscrupulous behavior. In 2003, for example, a number of US investment banks were found to have misled investors by encouraging them to buy shares that they themselves were underwriting, even though their own research departments thought the shares were poor value. Ten companies, including Merrill Lynch and the stockbroking arm of Citigroup, were fined a total of $1.4 billion.[9]

Casualties

The 2008 financial meltdown produced some spectacular casualties among the investment banks. They had been borrowing huge sums to trade on their own accounts, buying shares and other assets to take advantage of rising share and property prices. In 2007 the five independent US investment banks had borrowed between 25 and 35 times the value of their shareholders' equity in order to gamble on the markets.[10] When the markets started to collapse the lenders withdrew their funding, leaving the investment banks staring over a precipice.

In March 2008, 85-year-old Bear Stearns imploded and, chaperoned by the US government, was bought by the universal bank JPMorgan Chase for next to nothing. In September 2008, another bank, Lehman Brothers, got into deep trouble. This time however the government was less forgiving and, after trying to get Barclays and others to rescue it, decided to make an example of Lehman Brothers and let it go bust – owing a cool $613 billion and bequeathing the liquidator a rat's nest of transactions to unwind, making this one of the world's messiest ever bankruptcies. In the same month even the once mighty Merrill Lynch scurried to the shelter of a universal bank by selling itself to Bank of America for $50 billion. By the end of 2008 only Goldman Sachs and Morgan Stanley remained as self-standing investment banks. Whether they can survive in this form is questionable – given the inherent riskiness of the model. On the other hand, putting them inside commercial banks just transfers the hazards to ordinary bank customers who may unwittingly find themselves providing guarantees for reckless trading.[11]

Offshore financial centers and tax havens

The largest commercial banks usually have branches in many other countries. This is useful for customers who want to transact foreign business. But these banks may also have branches in small countries that have no significant trade – in what are called offshore financial centers (OFCs). In this case, however, their customers are generally looking for secrecy, politely referred to as 'discretion'. Such centers are not necessarily very far offshore. The UK, for example, has OFCs in the Channel Islands and the Isle of Man. Indeed the UK one way or another is responsible for a high proportion of OFCs since many, like Bermuda, the British Virgin Islands, or the Cayman Islands, are former colonies – and many are staffed by British expatriates.

Offshore centers are difficult to identify precisely. They may, for example, be thought of as places where most transactions are carried out by non-residents. However, this kind of activity is not confined to dodgy Caribbean jurisdictions. The City of London is a huge offshore financial center in that many of its customers live overseas.[12] Across the world there are thought to be 42 centers with significant offshore activities. These range from Hong Kong, with 454 licensed banks, to Belize with 5, or Vanuatu with 6.[13] According to a 2005 estimate by the Tax Justice Network, the world's high net worth individuals held around $11.5 trillion of assets offshore.[14]

The main purpose of this is to avoid taxes in the home country, a device which is thought to cost regular taxpayers worldwide at least $250 billion per year.

Banks of every shape and size

Not all offshore centers are tax havens, but most are. As defined by the OECD, a tax haven fulfills four criteria: an almost total lack of direct taxation; weak local economic activities; impenetrable tax rules; and a lack of disclosure of information to the tax authorities of other countries.

In the United Kingdom, for example, HM Revenue and Customs has estimated that in 2005 UK tax payers held around £80 billion offshore and that this was costing up to £1.5 billion in tax evasion. Favorite destinations were the Channel Islands, Switzerland, the Cayman Islands and the Isle of Man.[15] In the United States, Senator Carl Levin, testifying in 2007 before the Senate Finance Committee, said that tax evasion through offshore tax havens was costing the country as much as $100 billion per year.[16]

Offshore banks and companies are also useful for those engaged in illegal activities, particularly international organized crime and drug dealing, since tax havens are also ideal locations for money laundering. Criminals aiming to cloak the murky origins of their funds can set up webs of companies in multiple jurisdictions and transfer funds between various banks with different reporting requirements, making it hard to establish the electronic equivalent of a 'paper trail'.

Islamic banking
At the other end of the financial, and moral, spectrum from offshore banks are Islamic banks. According to sharia law, Muslims are forbidden from investing in unethical industries, such as liquor, gambling or pornography. Islam also requires its followers to use their wealth judiciously and not hoard it, and even forbids not just usurious rates of interest, but any interest at all.

This may appear a fatal restriction, but in practice Islamic banks achieve the same results through other means – generally by sharing profits and losses. If, for example, a customer wants a loan to buy a house or a car, the bank will buy the item and then resell it to the customer at a higher price, in installments over an agreed period. The price difference corresponds to what other banks would charge as interest.

They take a similar approach for savings accounts. When a customer makes a deposit, the bank invests this directly in businesses and then shares the profits with the customer. For customers, this has a further merit: these businesses have to comply with sharia law and refrain from unethical activities. This mechanism is thus also attractive for non-Muslims with similar moral scruples.

Globally this has become an increasingly important business. Since the mid-1990s Islamic banking has been growing by 10 per cent annually. At the end of 2006, Islamic financial services were worth around $530 billion globally, three quarters of which reflects activities of commercial banks.[17] Never slow to sniff out a financial opportunity, the City of London has now become a center for Islamic financial services with around $10 billion in sharia-compliant assets. Although London has been providing these for the past 30 years, it has now vastly increased its Islamic offerings and over 20 banks provide these services.

Deciding what is or is not compliant can be tricky. Islamic banks rely on boards of scholars who, for a suitable fee, act as a type of Islamic rating agency. At present, there is no final authority, though groups such as the Accounting and Auditing Organization for Islamic Financial Institutions are trying to establish global standards.

Microfinance
Another distinctive, and successful, form of banking that has come to the forefront in recent years has been microfinance. Although many countries have traditionally had village savings and loan associations, the

principles of modern microfinance were pioneered in Bangladesh from 1976 by Mohammad Yunus who established the Grameen (village) Bank in 1983 and won the 2006 Nobel Peace Prize for his achievements. The idea is simple. Poor people cannot usually get even tiny loans from banks because their business is too small and they can offer no security, no 'collateral'. Yunus realized however that the poor, and particularly women, were among the most careful users of money precisely because they had so little of it. He therefore replaced collateral with trust. In his microfinance scheme, women join together in small groups applying peer group pressure which can ensure strikingly high loan recovery rates – over 98 per cent. They can get micro-loans for productive self-employment, at close to market interest rates, repaying on a monthly or weekly basis. The women also have to make regular savings.

Once the money is repaid, members can take further loans. The women also get training and other support, including help with their children's education. Grameen Bank, which has 2,535 branches across Bangladesh, is a mutual organization, 95 per cent owned by its borrowers – all 7.6 million of them – and by 2006 had disbursed $7.4 billion in loans.[18]

In many microfinance schemes, borrowers gain access to funds through group lending so that if one member does not repay her loan, all the members suffer. The others may thus have to contribute to avoid being denied future loans. This represents a form of joint liability with a degree of self-screening, reducing the need for the lender to assess each individual too closely – which helps bring down costs. A survey of 146 groups in Madagascar, for example, found that the groups that performed best were those with stronger mutual ties and clear internal rules and regulations.[19]

Across the world, thousands of other microfinance institutions have sprung up. In the past, most were operated by non-governmental organizations, credit unions and other financial cooperatives or state-owned development banks. However, in recent years many commercial banks have spotted a profit opportunity and are organizing their own microfinance programs. This has created some controversy since Yunus and others believe that it is immoral to make money out of the poor, and that microfinanciers should accept very limited profits. Others however, particularly in Latin America, believe that it is important to bring in profit-orientated private investors to ensure that sufficient capital is available. Mexico's largest microfinance lender, for example, is Compartamos Banco, with more than 800,000 clients. This was set up with just $6 million in capital, but when it went public in 2007 it raised $450 million for its backers. This could be because of the fairly extortionate rates it charges – around 100 per cent annually. Microfinanciers are now being called upon to sign a code of ethics, the Pocantico Declaration, designed to ensure that microfinance, while it should be a profitable business, should also be grounded on firm ethical principles.[20]

Microfinance loans are generally for people to run their own businesses, which of course is not necessarily what the poorest people want to do; not everyone is an entrepreneur. And critics argue that small loans do little to lift people out of poverty. Nevertheless microfinance has certainly served as a vital safety net for the poor.

The credit genie

The world has thus found money, whether commodity money or fiat money, a useful device – making trade much more convenient. Banking too, in all its forms, has proved a remarkably successful innovation, especially given its difficult history. But once the credit genie is out of the bottle it can be difficult to control, opening up the prospect of bank failures and catastrophic collapse.

Microcredit takes off

By the end of 2005, some 1,333 microcredit institutions reported reaching 113 million clients. Bangladesh was still in the forefront; indeed Asia and the Pacific accounted for 96 million, but there were also 7 million clients in Sub-Saharan Africa and 4.4 million in Latin America and the Caribbean.* The graph below indicates the rapid growth of microfinance institutions. Around 70 per cent of loans globally go to the poorest people – those below national or international poverty lines.

*Daley-Harris, S 2006. *State of the Microcredit Summit Campaign Report.* www.microcreditsummit.org

Growth in microfinance, 1997-2005

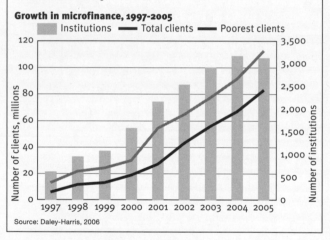

Source: Daley-Harris, 2006

Banks are also at the heart of capitalism. Indeed without businesses prepared to put money to work, banks would be unable to offer interest on loans. The ways in which companies raise bank loans and other funds are the subject of the next chapter.

1 EIU, 2008. *Country finance report, Brazil 2008.* London, Economist Intelligence Unit. 2 EIU, 2008. *Country finance report, Nigeria 2008.* London, Economist Intelligence Unit. 3 RB Australia, 1999. 'Demutualisation in Australia', *Reserve Bank of Australia Bulletin*, January. 4 RB Australia, 1999. 'Demutualisation in Australia', *Reserve Bank of Australia Bulletin*, January. 5 OTS, 2008. *Office of Thrift Supervision, Annual Report*, Washington, US Treasury. 6 FT, 2008. Washington Mutual, in *The Financial Times*, 26 September. 7 WOCCU, 2007. *Statistical report*, World Council

of Credit Unions, Madison WI. **8** EIU, 2008. *Financial Centres, Canada*, London, Economist Intelligence Unit. **9** EIU, 2008. *Financial Centres, USA*, London, Economist Intelligence Unit. **10** *The Economist*, 2008. 'Special report on international banking. Paradise lost', in The Economist, 15 May. **11** *The Economist*, 2008. 'Is there a future?', in The Economist 18 September. **12** McGuire, P and N Tarashev, 2008. *Global monitoring with the BIS international banking statistics*, BIS Working Papers No 244 by Monetary and Economic Department. **13** IMF, 2000. *Offshore Financial Centers*, IMF Background Paper. **14** TJN, 2005. *The Price of Offshore*, Tax Justice Network Briefing Paper. **15** HMRC, 2005. *Estimation of tax gap for direct taxes*, KAI Analysis, 8 – Compliance Strategy. London, HM Revenue and Customs. **16** Levin C. 2007. *Statement of Senator Carl Levin before the Senate Finance Committee on Offshore Tax Evasion: Stashing Cash Overseas*. http://www.senate.gov/~levin/newsroom/release.cfm?id=275085 **17** IFSL, 2008. *Banking 2008*. London, International Financial Services. Ifsl.org.uk **18** Grameen Bank, 2008. www.grameen.com **19** Hermes N. and R Lensink, 2007. 'The Empirics of Microfinance: what do we know?', in *The Economic Journal*, 117 (February), F1–F10. (Blackwell Publishing, Oxford). **20** Blakely, R. 2008. 'Microfinance raises fresh sub-prime fears' in *The Times*, 14 July.

4 Capital casinos

The objective of banks and other financial institutions is simple – to connect savers and investors and put money to work in such a way that everyone is aware of the benefits and the risks. But the techniques have become increasingly complex. From issuing stocks and bonds, the financial markets have moved on to ever more arcane 'derivatives' that are making the real risks almost impossible to assess – and placing the world's financial system in jeopardy.

ALTHOUGH YOU EARN money as cash, if this accumulates you have to decide what to do with it. If you stuff banknotes under your mattress, you might feel on top of your finances. But in addition to risking burglary and some uncomfortable sleeping positions you could be wasting an opportunity because if you save it in a bank you should be able to earn some interest, perhaps around 5 per cent per year. The mattress option also exposes you to the risks of inflation, because $100 withdrawn from your mattress one year later is likely to be worth at least 2 or 3 per cent less in terms of goods than it was when you first earned it. In the UK, for example, between 1997 and 2007 inflation averaged 2.3 per cent per year. This means that over those 10 years the value of £1 fell to 72 pence.[1] You will probably therefore choose to put it in a bank where it will earn interest, and hopefully overcome the effects of inflation.

The bank can afford to pay you interest because it is going to lend most of your money to someone else who is going to pay them even more interest, of say 7 per cent per year. The bank pockets the difference to cover its expenses and deliver profit to its owners. Usually as a saver you will get better interest rates if you are prepared to leave your money undisturbed for long periods. If you want to be able to withdraw instantly you will get a lower rate than if you are prepared to

Keeping ahead of inflation

Getting interest from your savings should help protect you from inflation. This graphic shows the difference between the base interest rate set by the Bank of England and the annual inflation rates. The rates for deposits for banks and building societies are typically one or two percentage points above the base rate. For almost all of this period, interest rates have exceeded inflation rates – which is comforting for savers, though in fact any interest would be better than none at all.

Interest and inflation rates, UK, 1975-2007

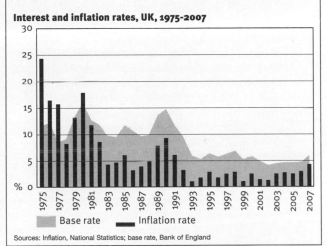

Base rate   Inflation rate

Sources: Inflation, National Statistics; base rate, Bank of England

give notice of one month, say, or one year. This gives the bank greater freedom to lend for a longer period with less risk that you and other depositors will show up all wanting to withdraw at the same time.

Ultimately, however, both the bank and you are only being paid interest because someone is putting your money to work. This can happen in many ways, of which the most obvious is a bank loan to a small business. The person who finishes up with your money might, for example, be a shopkeeper who wants to fill her store with goods but does not have enough ready cash to do so. She can, however, take a loan from the bank that can steadily be repaid as the goods are sold.

Capital casinos

Of course saving with a bank also brings risks. The bank itself could go bust if its borrowers renege, and your money can disappear with it. When deciding where to deposit your funds, you always have to balance income and security; generally the higher the interest rate, the lower the security.

However in the case of banks the risks for most depositors are quite low. The government will usually offer an official guarantee: either it will bail out the bank if it gets into trouble, or at the very least it will establish systems of insurance that offer protection to small savers. The financial meltdown of 2008 had governments scurrying to increase the amount on which savers could rely. In the United States, the amount insured per depositor per bank was increased from $100,000 to $250,000. In Canada, in late 2008, the amount was C$100,000. The British government in 2008 increased the amount from £35,000 to £50,000.

Buying into business

Passing on your money in the form of a loan to someone else via a bank is of course only one way in which you can use your savings to earn money. You have many other options. You could, for example, buy an enterprise yourself. If your shopkeeper is very successful, or just wants to retire, he or she could simply sell the business. How much should you pay? You might think that all you need do is add up its various components: the value of the building, the fixtures and fittings and the stock. But it is unlikely that the owner would consider this to be fair. After all, the shopkeeper has done all the work of getting everything running smoothly and acquiring regular customers, so he or she would also want the price to reflect the fact that you would be buying a going concern. But how can you set a price on such imponderables?

The simplest way is to ask how much profit the business is earning. Let's assume it has a manager in place and all you would have to do is put up the funds and take the profits after all salaries and other expenses had been paid. According to her accounts, let's say the shop owner is making a profit of $50,000 per year. How much would you be prepared to invest to earn that? If banks were offering a long-term interest rate of five per cent then to earn $50,000 in interest you would have to deposit one $1 million – quite a lot. Should you pay $1 million?

Probably not. This is usually a riskier proposition than putting money in a bank. Lots of things could go wrong and you will have no guarantees. Generally, therefore you would offer less than this, probably competing with other buyers who are also making similar judgments. Of course, there is also the possibility that you think you could make the business even more profitable, by selling different goods, or by turning the prime location into a café. Nevertheless, the basic principle remains the same: you have to assess future profits and bid for the business accordingly.

Equity options

As you probably don't have a million dollars to spare, or do not want the hassle of owning the whole business, you might prefer to buy only a part. The idea of selling shares in businesses has a long history. During the Renaissance, groups of merchants would get together to invest in the ships needed for particular voyages. But the first permanent business owned by shareholders was the Dutch East India Company in the 17th century.

Nowadays, starting a limited company involves issuing a certain number of shares – which can be as few as two. At the outset these are typically owned by the founder or the immediate family, or may be given to employees. Nevertheless this is still considered a private company. In fact, many huge corporations are still privately owned. Cargill, for example, which is one of the world's largest agribusiness corporations, is joint-ly owned by members of the Cargill and MacMillan families. And Mars, which supplies the world with Twix, M&Ms and Snickers – among other delights – is owned by members of the Mars family. In the US in 2004, the 339 companies that were privately owned sold around $1 trillion-worth of goods and services and employed 4 million people.[2]

In Europe one of the largest private companies is IKEA. It is controlled, via a complex tax avoidance scheme, and a rather ungenerous charity, by Ingvar Kamprad, who founded the company aged 17 in 1944 as a door-to-door supplier of nylon stockings and wallets. In 2004 the company was worth around $58 billion.[3] Many companies prefer to remain private since they do not have to disclose many of the details of their opera-tions, and can function more independently, perhaps with a longer-term vision.

Most of the larger companies, however, eventually choose to sell their shares to the public through stock exchanges. Perhaps the company needs to raise funds for expansion, or maybe the founders want to cash in on their success. At this point they will make an 'ini-tial public offering'. Setting the price of the shares is tricky since the worth of a business is determined not by just the bricks and mortar of its factories and offices but by its potential for generating profits in the future. At this point the company will usually call on the ser-vices of an investment bank which, for a sizeable fee (one to two per cent), will advise the company on the initial share price and assist in the flotation.

Usually this involves the investment bank putting its money where its mouth is by 'underwriting' the share issue – that is, it promises to buy any unsold shares – though it will normally disperse the risk by assembling an ad hoc syndicate. In August 2007, for example, Cosan, Brazil's largest producer of sugar and ethanol fuel alternatives, issued $1 billion-worth of shares.

Swiss banking giant Credit Suisse acted as the lead underwriter.[4] Although in theory such sales are open to everyone, in practice the investment bank will usually allocate shares to favored institutions that give them regular business.

Pop go the prices

On the first day's trading there is usually a sudden 'pop' as the shares jump to a higher value and the favored investors can pocket a quick profit. For example, at the height of the dotcom bubble in 1999-2000, investment banks raked in $7.3 billion from advising in various offerings. But the 'money left on the table' as a result of the multiple pops was $66 billion some of which was certainly quietly shared with the investment banks.[5]

One company that tried in 2004 to cut the bankers out of this lucrative loop and give the small investor a chance was Google. It set its share price instead through a 'Dutch auction', asking potential buyers how many shares they wanted and what they were prepared to pay.

The highest bidders were allocated all the shares they asked for, as were the bidders below them, until all the shares were exhausted. The share price was set as the one offered by the lowest successful bidder – $85. Even so, the shares still popped to $100 on the first day's trading and anyone who did get shares would have done quite well: they reached $700 each in 2007, though by early 2009 were down to $325.

Once the company has gone public it then has the resources to swallow up other ones. In Australia, for example, law firms, which previously were partnerships, are now allowed to sell shares to the public. One major firm, Slater & Gordon, went public in 2007 and within a year had used the funds to gobble up six smaller rivals. Since the initial public offering, the firm's share price has risen 50 per cent. Companies flush with flotation cash can also use this to poach the best staff from other companies.[6]

Watching the share price

The terms shares and stocks are often used interchangeably – 'shares' is generally used in the UK and 'stocks' in North America, but in both cases they are traded in stock exchanges and are also known as 'equities'. Share prices can be very volatile since a company's perceived prospects can be shaped by many factors. Investors will look not just at its current profitability or the extent of its assets, but will also be swayed by rumors about future products, for example, or management changes.

As a shareholder you are now a part-owner and can vote for members of the board of directors. You are also entitled to any annual 'dividend'. If the company makes a profit it can choose to distribute this to shareholders. On the other hand it may decide to retain the profits to invest in the business. In that case the value of the business, and thus the share price, should go up.

A business that sells shares gets the advantage of an injection of capital, but at the cost of a loss of control. A company that was happy to run itself for the benefit of its original owners or its workers, or even its customers, is now legally obliged to consider the interests of shareholders – which are often quite different. Shareholders are generally preoccupied with seeing the value of the holdings rise and in reaping annual dividends. They want to see a profit on their investment and are likely to fire directors, or through them any managers, whom they think are costing them money. Moreover, if the share price collapses the company becomes ripe for a takeover. A low share price may allow a predator, often a competitor, to buy up a company very cheaply. The least popular purchasers, however, are the 'asset strippers' who will 'buy, strip and flip' a company then sell off its assets, making a substantial profit.

In practice you are more likely to own shares indirectly. Around half of US publicly traded shares are owned by institutions, such as pension funds, and the rest by individual investors. In the UK, institutions are even more dominant, controlling more than two-thirds of listed shares.[7] Managing such funds is a huge business. Insurance companies or pension funds have their own fund managers. But there are also funds which gather investments from individual, or 'retail' customers who pool their resources with other investors, into what are called unit trusts in the UK and mutual funds in the US. In the UK, in mid 2008, there were 2,223 investment funds, run by 108 companies, managing £450 billion in assets.[8]

What do they do with this money? Firms like Gartmore, PDFM, Schroders and Mercury in the UK put 70 to 80 per cent of their money into shares, two-thirds of this in the domestic market, and invest the rest in bonds or keep it as cash. Most of these funds will claim to manage your money better than the average investor – that they will outperform the market. But of course all of them cannot. Indeed they tend to do rather worse. Between 1984 and 2002, a period when the value of the top 500 companies in the US grew by 13 per cent a year, the average equity mutual fund returned only around 10 per cent.[9] For all the expertise they claim, success is mostly a matter of luck. Nevertheless, as long as the market is rising most will look vaguely competent. Some will also reduce the risks of looking bad by not actively managing funds at all but simply buying shares that match those in the standard stock exchange indices. By definition these passive 'tracker funds' should not be too disastrous.

Private equity
One of the most striking developments in recent years is the emergence of predatory private equity firms. These are enterprises which buy up other companies,

either public or private, on the assumption that they can manage the companies better and eventually sell them on for a profit. Typically they do this by borrowing large sums from banks and then buying up all the company's shares which are then removed from the stock exchange. Private equity companies are usually themselves private companies, or owned by other financial firms. One exception is the large private equity company Blackstone, which went public in June 2007.

When a company takes over a business using borrowed funds it is carrying out a 'leveraged buyout', anticipating that it can pay off the debt when it reorganizes and resells the company at a profit. Blackstone carried out one of the largest ever deals when in 2006 it bought America's largest commercial landlord, Equity Office Properties, for $39 billion. Since this was less than the properties were worth, within months Blackstone was able to break up the company, selling most of the properties and making a tidy profit.[10]

Many private equity operators have become fabulously wealthy. Steve Schwarzman, the founder of Blackstone, is worth $6.4 billion. Reportedly, he spent $3 million for his 60th birthday party, which involved paying $1 million for a personal appearance by Rod Stewart. Even he was outdone by another private equity mogul, David Bonderman of the company TPG, who is thought to be worth $3 billion, and spent $10 million for his birthday, though he preferred the Rolling Stones.[11]

The credit crunch has put the brakes on many private equity firms. Although they have plenty of their own capital they prefer to make most of their bids using bank loans. Many have been caught owning companies whose value has crashed and they now find it very difficult to service or renew the loans.

Buying bonds

Another way to raise funds for a business is to sell bonds. A bond is a financial contract in which the seller promises to pay the buyer a fixed rate of interest and after a certain period to repay the whole sum. The idea of bonds arose in the Middle Ages when monarchs wanted to borrow large sums to finance wars. When they had run out of wealthy individuals they could tap, they divided their requests into smaller amounts by issuing bonds that could be bought by many other citizens. Some of the first bonds are thought to have been issued in Venice in 1157 to finance a war with Constantinople.[12] Bonds issued by governments are assumed to be very safe since governments cannot go bust in their own currencies – they always have the option of raising more taxes or printing more money.

Bonds issued by companies are inherently more risky, though when issued by large companies are usually considered 'investment grade'. Bonds were used, for example, to finance transcontinental railroads in the United States in the 19th century. Companies building infrastructure often sell bonds to help finance the huge upfront costs – and pay the interest and eventually the principal with the income from fares and freight charges. As with equities, bonds are usually issued on the advice of investment banks. They may either be sold directly to institutional or corporate investors or placed publicly, in which case the company has to issue a prospectus which says what the funds are to be used for, when the bond will be redeemed, and what rate of interest will be offered.

Corporations usually issue bonds that run from six to ten years. If they want money for shorter periods, up to three months, they issue an equivalent of bonds called 'commercial paper'. In the past, all bonds were issued as paper certificates and incorporated a set of coupons that could be torn off to collect each six-monthly payment. Nowadays most bonds are electronic transactions but for the payment the term 'coupon' persists.

Bonds differ from shares in that generally they do

not confer any control over the company. However, like shares they can subsequently be bought and sold – in the bond market. And just as with shares the resale price can fluctuate. One reason for fluctuations is that the issuing corporation may get into difficulties and be considered a bad credit risk. But the main sources of volatility are changes in interest rates.

To see why interest rates affect bond resale prices, suppose that at a time when interest rates are 3 per cent you buy a $1,000 ten-year bond from IBM which has a coupon, corresponding to an interest rate, of 5 per cent. That seems like a good deal – two percentage points higher than the prevailing interest rates. But interest rates fluctuate while the coupon on the bond is fixed at the outset. After a couple of years, interest rates might for example rise to 6 per cent, while your bond still has a coupon of only 5 per cent. This will make no difference to you unless you try to sell the bond. If you do, you will now find, however, that it is worth less. If a potential buyer wanted to get a yield two percentage points above the prevailing interest rate they would have to either buy a new bond with an 8 per cent coupon or, to achieve the same result they might offer to buy your bond for $620 – quite a drop. In this case the buyer will be considering the 'yield' which is the coupon divided by the current market price.

Of course the coupon, which is effectively the interest rate paid on the bond, is not the only factor, since the bond will eventually be redeemed for $1,000 and the closer you get to the redemption date the more you would get for it even at a time of high interest rates. Conversely if interest rates fall then the market value of your bond goes up – and the company that issued it will be locked into paying a coupon which is higher than the prevailing interest rates. If you simply hang on to your bond you can ignore these fluctuations, safe in the knowledge that IBM will give you $50 per year and eventually return your $1,000 'principal', ie initial investment – though, after ten years, inflation would have made the principal worth a lot less.

Corporate bonds typically have higher yields than government bonds. In Canada, for example, in April 2008, the average yield on top-rated ten-year bonds issued by the major banks was 5.6 per cent, compared with 3.6 per cent for Government of Canada bonds.[13] Unlike shares, bonds are not generally traded in exchanges but directly, either between buyers and sellers or via dealers in what are termed 'over-the-counter' trades.

Junk bonds

Bonds are also issued by companies which are less solid than IBM, which still seems to be in reasonable shape. But since their bonds are considered riskier, they have to tempt buyers by offering higher coupons. Buyers who want to check on these bonds can consult credit rating agencies such as Moody's or Standard and Poor's which apply ratings – from AAA to CCC. In the past, around half of bonds rated CCC by these agencies have defaulted within six years. Bonds rated B- and below are considered 'high yield' or speculative, and are referred to as 'junk' bonds. In recent years these have offered coupons 8 percentage points above comparable investment-grade bonds.[14]

The ratings offered by the agencies are of course only their opinions, and they make mistakes. As elsewhere in financial markets, there is considerable margin for error – and consequently profit. In the past the sellers of junk bonds have often been more generous than they needed to be – or the buyers have been unduly skeptical. As a result, junk bonds have offered better yields than merited by the actual risk. One person who capitalized on this in the 1980s was Michael Milken who worked at the investment bank Drexel Burnham Lambert. He started to buy up bonds whose ratings had slipped and made a fortune in the process when they came good. Then Drexel Burnham Lambert and others who wanted to raise money to finance take-over bids started to issue their own junk bonds. At his peak, Milken the 'junk bond king' was raking in $500 million per year, but he sailed too close to the wind once too often and in 1989 was jailed for two years for racketeering and fraud.

Corporate bonds come in all sorts of varieties, which you probably don't need to know about so you can skip the rest of this paragraph. But just to give a flavor, some – the 'callables' – allow the issuer to re-call them before redemption, which is useful if interest rates fall. Others, the 'puttables', can be returned by the owner before maturing. Some have floating rates, while others, the 'zero-coupons' have no yield at all and instead are sold at the outset for prices less than the redemption rates.

Asset-backed bonds

Most of these complexities are of interest only to bond traders but one variety which does have a wider significance for the current financial meltdown is the 'asset-backed' bond. This is akin to a share since in the event of default the owner has a degree of ownership, if not of the company as a whole at least of something that it produces or owns. A recent example is a mortgage bond backed by property that could be sold off in the event of a default. Chapter 8 will explain in greater detail how this kind of insecure security triggered the financial meltdown of 2008.

Investors who have the choice of buying equities or bonds have difficult decisions to make as prices and interest rates change. But over the longer term equities have proved more profitable. Researchers at the London Business School have found that over the past century investments in equities delivered 4 per cent more per year than bonds, which may not seem like much but eventually accumulates to a very large sum[15].

Government bonds and national debt

The safest bonds to invest in are those issued by governments, particularly in the richer developed countries which are good credit risks because they cannot go bust: if the worst comes to the worst, governments can pay back by raising taxes or just printing more money. Government bonds, referred to as 'sovereign' debt, go under a number of different names in the issuing countries. In the US, they are called Treasuries, while in the UK they are called gilts. Local governments can also issue bonds, though these are typically backed by national authorities. In Canada, for example, each of the ten provinces can issue debt to finance its own initiatives.

In the past, governments in developed countries often issued bonds to pay for large infrastructure projects such as highways or bridges. This is considered a way to promote 'intergenerational equity' since taking the funds from current taxes would not only be unpopular, it would involve charging people who may get little benefit in their lifetimes. Nowadays, however, governments issue bonds primarily to balance the difference between income and expenditure – to finance a budget deficit. Public debt is thus largely the accumulated deficit, which is held as bonds and other forms of securities by corporations, individuals, or within other parts of the government system.

Many people have become very alarmed at the scale of their national debts, and have issued public warnings – notably through digital National Debt 'clocks'. The 13-digit clock in Times Square in New York City has been ticking since the early 1980s. After the $700 billion bail-out of the banks in 2008, the debt spiraled beyond $10 trillion and the clock ran out of digits. A new clock is planned with 15 digits to permit a debt of one quadrillion dollars. $10.5 trillion amounts to $31,500 per US citizen. If you are feeling in a generous mood, the US Treasury invites public contributions to reduce the debt – please make your checks payable to the 'Bureau of the Public Debt'.[16]

In the event of the government earning more from taxes than it spends, it can reduce the debt itself by buying back its own bonds. Australia has had some success at this and by 2006 had eliminated its official government debt.[17] Canada has also been trying to pay off its debt which between 1996 and 2006 fell from 71 to 33 per cent of GDP. Even so, federal debt is still Can\$472 billion, around Can\$14,000 per person.

In the United Kingdom the 2008/09 deficit was planned to be around 2.1 per cent. The budget forecast for net debt at the end of September 2008 was £645 billion, thus a little over £1,000 per person.[18] However, as a result of the financial meltdown the British government suddenly decided to cut taxes and increase expenditure, roughly doubling the annual deficit.

For the richer Western countries, sovereign debt seems alarming but can eventually be repaid. But other countries may not be so reliable. In 1998, Russia faced a collapse of the ruble and informed its bond holders, domestic and foreign, that it was not going to repay – leading, among other things, to the collapse of a huge US hedge fund Long Term Capital Management, which had been speculating in Russian bonds.

Many developing countries have had much more alarming debt experiences. Most do have some domestic debt, having sold bonds to their national companies or institutions. If these bonds are in the national currency, this is less of a problem. But because their currencies are weak, and their credit records shaky, developing country governments and companies often borrow overseas in other currencies, usually dollars. Sometimes this has been in the form of bonds, where the interest rates are usually fixed, but more often through the riskier route of commercial bank loans at variable rates. A number of developing countries have defaulted on sovereign debt, most notably Argentina

Argentina's lenders take a haircut

As a result of an economic crisis in 2001, Argentina could no longer service its debts and decided to default. Then in 2004 it offered to swap its defaulted bonds, worth $81 billion, for new ones worth only $35 billion. The bonds were held by financial institutions at home and abroad, as well as by many individual investors in Japan and Europe. Most accepted the offer and thus lost around half their money – known as 'taking a haircut'. Others, who held around $20-billion-worth refused the deal. As a result Argentina's name remains mud in international capital markets so it cannot borrow there*. Instead it has had to rely on other governments – such as that of Venezuela's Hugo Chávez, who by mid-2008 had bought $7 billion in Argentinean bonds, the latest of which had to pay interest rates of 15 per cent.**

*EIU, 2008. Argentina, Country Profile. London, Economist Intelligence Unit.

**The Economist, 2008. 'Clouds gather again over the Pampas', in The Economist, 23 August.

(see box *Argentina's lenders take a haircut*).

Thirty years ago bonds were considered safe investments, but rather dull. Now buyers have a Ben and Jerry's type array of bonds flavors to choose from. And they can use complex mathematical models to exploit very small differences in the yields of similar bonds. Much more exciting.

Derivatives

Much of the current financial chaos has arisen, however, not as a result of trading directly in shares or bonds, but in what are termed 'derivatives' – contracts which are derived from, or based on, shares or bonds or some other financial instrument. While stock markets generally have been likened to casinos, the use of derivatives ratchets the betting element to much higher levels.

When used in moderation, derivatives work like insurance policies. Many companies or institutions nervous about market volatility will buy or sell derivatives to protect or 'hedge' themselves. But when used recklessly, they can be very dangerous. Derivatives can take many complex and bizarre forms, known as 'exotics', but the plain-vanilla ones are relatively

---

Futures and options

Companies often worry that while they have to make long term production plans, the prices of what they buy or sell will subsequently
turn against them. If so, they can enter into a futures contract – an
agreement to buy or sell something at a later date but at a price that
is fixed now. Futures trading has a long history. In the 16th century, for
example, fish dealers in Holland were buying and selling prospective
catches of herring. But by the 19th century this had developed into
standardized contracts after the Chicago Board of Trade introduced
futures trading in grain. In a more recent example, airline companies
use futures to buy aviation fuel. Instead of just buying it on a daily
basis they enter into a contract to buy fuel at a certain price, say three
or six months hence. At times this has served them well. During 2008,
they were hedged at around $80 per barrel of oil when the actual
price peaked at over $150, before falling again to below $50. If you
buy a future you are obliged to purchase the item on the due date, or
sell it to someone else. However, you can also buy an 'option' which
gives you the right, but not the obligation, to buy or sell something at
a specific price in the future. Whether or not you take up the option,
you still have to pay up front for the privilege – which might add 10 to
20 per cent to the final price.

---

straightforward. The simplest include 'futures' which
allow buyers or sellers to buffer themselves against
future price changes by locking their transaction to
current prices (see box *Futures and options*).

Others involve various kinds of exchange known as
'swaps' (see box *An interest in swapping*), of which one
of the riskiest is a 'credit default swap' which played a
major part in the 2008 financial meltdown (see box
Gambling with risk, p78).

While many companies use derivatives to provide security, others – which have no need of say barrels of
oil, or pork bellies, or cotton – use derivatives primarily
as vehicles for speculation. This is a high-risk occupa-
tion, particularly for sellers who do not actually own
the item. Normally to buy a 'future', for example, the
buyer needs only to deposit a part, perhaps 10 per cent,
of the final payment; so for relatively small sums buyers
can expose themselves to very large losses – or gains.

In most cases the volume of trading in derivatives

An interest in swapping

Swaps seem rather unlikely forms of derivative but are used quite frequently. A common one is an interest rate swap. For example one company which has a ten-year loan at a fixed interest rate could swap this with another company that has a similar loan but at a floating interest rate. Through a swap contract each agrees to pay the other's interest charges. Why would anyone want to do this? Generally it is because the two parties know more about each other than does the market. If, for example, a US company wants to expand in Europe where it is not well known and wants a loan in euros it may have to accept one from a European bank at an unfavorable floating rate. It may therefore make a swap with a French company that is in a position to negotiate a better, fixed rate.

far exceeds the trade in the underlying commodity. For while there is a limit to how much wheat is available, for example, there need be no limit to the number of futures contracts based on its price. Many of these contracts are written by speculators who may be praised for providing a valuable service to those who really do need to hedge their position – or condemned as unproductive parasites who are exploiting the markets for reckless gambling. Take your pick.

Hedge funds

Much of the speculative trading in derivatives is carried out by 'hedge' funds. These are so called because originally they were a means of hedging against the risk of sudden market slumps. Nowadays this is a serious misnomer since these funds are used not for achieving security but for high-stakes speculation.

You can think of hedge funds as mutual funds for the rich. In the US, hedge funds will not let you through the front door unless you are prepared to invest at least $1 million and can demonstrate an income of more than $200,000 per year. Some will also lock up your money for five years.

Typically they work on a very lucrative 'two and 20' basis, charging investors around 2 per cent of the

Gambling with risk – speculating with credit default swaps

This is one of the newest forms of derivatives, though it is less obviously a swap and more a kind of insurance policy for holders of bonds or other volatile assets. The coupon on a bond, for example, is based on two considerations. The first is the prevailing interest rate in the market; the second is the risk that the borrower will default. The dodgier the borrower, the higher the risk element and thus the higher the coupon rate. A more cautious lender can pay someone else to remove the risk of default, for an annual premium – a 'credit default swap' (CDS). Companies selling this insurance may indeed be insurance companies, but banks and other institutions will also sell CDSs. Note that this does not entirely remove the risk, since the insurance company could also go bust – a hazard known as 'counterpart' risk.

Suppose you have bought $10 million worth of bonds from Transnational Airways Inc. that have a yield of 5 per cent – earning you $500,000 per year. Instead, you could have bought government bonds with a yield of only 2 per cent. This means that you are being rewarded for the risk element in Transnational with another 3 percentage points. In the financial jargon this is referred to as a 'spread' of 300 basis points.

But then you get cold feet. You could either rush off and sell the bond or you could just sell the risk element, say to the Acme Insurance Corp. At 3 per cent of $10 million that would cost you $300,000 per year. If Transnational Airways remains in financial good health and continues to pay the coupon throughout the life of the swap contract then nothing happens. Acme simply pockets the premiums just as it would for any other policy for which a claim is never made. If, on the other hand, Transnational crashes to earth, then Acme has to pay you $10 million – though you still lose your premiums.

But that is much too simple. Speculators have seized on the credit default swap as a means of betting on the fragile financial health of Transnational Inc. Anyone can buy insurance on Transnational's bonds whether they own them or not. Acme is happy to sell CDSs to all comers. If Transnational goes bust, then those who do actually have the bonds will get their full value. Speculators who do not have any actual bonds still get paid, but not the $10 million. If, as a result of the bankruptcy, Transnational's bonds are being repaid by the liquidators at only 30 per cent of their value, then all you can claim from Acme is $7 million.

Who uses hedge funds?

Around one-third of investment in hedge funds comes from 'high-net-worth' individuals, but a high proportion now comes from 'funds of hedge funds' which are designed to enable others to invest indirectly by dispersing their money across a variety of hedge funds. Part of your pension may well be invested by an institution in a hedge fund.* By the end of 2008, there were around 7,000 such funds, managing $1.9 trillion in assets. Around two-thirds of hedge funds are in the US, though Europe and Asia are gaining ground.

* *The Economist*, 2008. 'The incredible shrinking funds', in *The Economist*, 25 October.

Investors in hedge funds, 2008

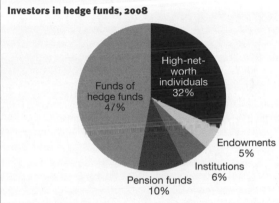

Source: *The Economist*, 2008

assets managed, but also taking 20 per cent of any profits. This can make managers very rich, and during the 1990s the most successful mutual fund managers jumped ship to work for hedge funds. One leading fund in the UK is Odey Asset Management whose 12 partners manage assets worth £2.7 billion. In 2007/08 they made £55 million in profit, with Mr Odey himself taking home £28 million. The secret of his success, he says, is 'paranoia'.[19]

Hedge funds follow a variety of strategies. Unlike mutual funds which aim largely just to keep ahead of the market, hedge funds are aiming for much higher 'absolute returns'. And while mutual funds usually only get good returns in a rising market, hedge funds can also make money in falling markets. They do this by 'shorting' shares they think will fall in value. This involves selling shares they do not actually own. Instead they 'rent' the shares, from a pension fund say, sell them at their current price, and buy them back later, hopefully at a lower price, so they can hand the same number of shares back to the lender. If the share price goes up, however, they will lose. Betting on corporate failure in this way allows hedge funds to keep ahead of the game. During the last big financial collapse following the dotcom implosion, shares in the US fell by one third but the value of the average hedge fund stayed roughly flat.[20]

Scenting blood

On the other hand there can be disastrous consequences for the companies whose shares they target. Once hedge funds smell blood in the water they can drive even potentially viable companies into a downward spiral. To protect the markets in some countries the authorities have been banning short selling. In July 2008, for example, the US Securities and Exchange Commission introduced new regulation to control dishonest 'naked' short selling – the sale of shares one has not yet even borrowed, by taking advantage of the period between the sale of the stock and the time it has to be delivered.[21]

In addition to short selling, hedge funds may also engage in frantic trading. In May 2008 one trader in a London-based hedge fund, GLG, bought and sold his $5 billion fund portfolio 56 times, almost three times a day – to make a 5 per cent return. His brokers would not have complained, having earned a tasty $600 million in commissions.[22] While some would argue that this lubricates the markets, it can also make them very volatile. As a result of all this activity, hedge funds account for a high proportion of trading. In 2006, they are thought to have accounted for 35 to 50 per cent of trading volumes in the British and American stock exchanges and around 60 per cent of trading on credit derivatives.[23]

As well as having human beings buying and selling, hedge funds can also use computers to make instant trades using software. These quantitative funds, the 'quants' may, for example, tell the computer to watch for tiny variations in the price of the same stock in London and New York, or make assessments based on standard indicators of past and present performance. This can yield rich returns but is also hazardous, especially when a herd of computers using similar software and data all press their own 'sell' keys simultaneously and dump vast quantities of the same stocks onto unsuspecting markets.

Juicy returns

Hedge funds can provide spectacular returns and juicy incomes for their managers. Two partners in GLG, for example, each trousered $350 million in 2007. But these funds can also come spectacularly unstuck. This is because they carry out much of their trading using borrowed funds. Hedge funds do not just use the funds from their investors to rent shares, they also borrow huge sums from the money markets. If you make a profit of 5 per cent on a $1 million deal this will net you only $50,000. Hardly worth getting out of bed for. But if for the same deal you have also borrowed $10 million, then the profit for the investor will be around $500,000. This way of amplifying returns with borrowed funds is termed 'leverage'. Indeed, investors expect their funds to be leveraged in this way to achieve high profits. Of course the corollary of this is that if the outcome is a 5 per cent loss, then you will lose $500,000. Overall, the industry's average leverage in 2008 was around three times its equity, which means that these companies were handling around $6 trillion.

Capital casinos

The hazards of leveraged hedge funds piloted even by the cleverest human beings were first brought home by the crash in 1998 of a US hedge fund, Long Term Capital Management (LTCM). This was the last occasion when the world's financial house of cards threatened to collapse. Founded in 1993, by high-flyer John Meriwether, the company's partners included two Nobel Prize winners in economics. LTCM was a 'relative value' trader, taking advantage of the fact that before their prices settle down newly issued bonds tend to have slightly higher values than older ones. The differences might be minuscule, one tenth of one per cent, but if you trade with around $25 million dollars at a time you can rake in $25,000 several times a day for not much work.

However, when you are employing vast amounts of other people's money and things go wrong, they do so in spectacular fashion. In traders' parlance, relative value funds 'eat like chickens, but shit like elephants'. LTCM came to grief in mid-1998 by buying huge quantities of Russian bonds only to be told shortly afterwards by the Russian government that it was blithely defaulting on all of them. *Niet*. After a couple of weeks of general panic, LTCM, whose shareholder capital was only $1 billion, owed around $100 billion and was spectacularly insolvent. The Federal Reserve became alarmed that if LTCM was forced to dump all its bonds onto the market the international financial system would collapse. So it banged some heads together and got 25 banks to mount a rescue. The Fed might also have wanted to disguise just how incompetent the banks had been in lending LTCM billions of dollars with little idea of what they were doing with them. Perhaps if the Fed had allowed LTCM to collapse then the banks might have learned their lesson and cleaned up their act. Incidentally, if you are anxious about the fate of Mr Meriwether you will be relieved to know that he was able to start another hedge fund, JWM Partners, which today manages around $2.6 billion in investor funds.[24]

Investing in hedge funds is not for the faint-hearted. Governments assume that people putting their money in hedge funds know what they are doing, so do not apply the same regulatory standards as they would for a company dealing with consumers. In the UK hedge funds are not allowed to advertise to the general public. If you are nevertheless excited by the prospect you can use some of your savings to invest in a 'fund of funds', in some cases as little as $25,000. But this may not be a good time to take the plunge. In fact many hedge fund investors are heading out of the door. Since hedge funds now find it more difficult to borrow funds they cannot achieve as much leverage, and bans on short selling will cut off one of their main routes to profit. The smaller funds, with less than $500 million, will find it difficult to survive.

Sovereign wealth funds

Another striking development on the global financial scene in recent years is the emergence of 'sovereign wealth funds'. These are investment funds controlled by governments that have amassed surpluses of money which they want to invest beyond their own shores. This rings all sorts of alarm bells. If you are nervous about seeing local companies bought up by foreign multinationals, how about having them controlled by foreign governments such as those in Russia or China or Saudi Arabia, which may manipulate these companies for their own political purposes?

Globally, sovereign wealth funds control around $2.9 trillion and are growing rapidly. The ten largest are indicated in the graphic *Sovereign wealth fund assets*.[25] Where does all this money come from? Most of the older funds, such as those in the United Arab Emirates (UAE), Norway, Saudi Arabia, and Kuwait, are the accumulations of oil revenues. Countries aware that they are exhausting natural resources put some of the proceeds into these funds as ways of saving for future generations.

This is also the case for smaller funds such as Canada's Alberta Heritage Savings Trust Fund, and the US's Alaska Permanent Fund. Others are 'stabilization funds' which the exporting countries use to smooth the impact of volatile commodity prices. Others, including those of China and Singapore, are derived from trade surpluses. Ironically some of the funds – in Malaysia and Australia, for example – were established with the proceeds of privatizations, so while the state may have been selling assets at home it has actually been part-nationalizing foreign companies.

Sovereign wealth funds have been around for a long time – the Kuwait Investment Fund, for example, was established in 1953. But for decades these funds did not

Sovereign wealth fund assets

Sovereign wealth funds are investment funds controlled by governments that have amassed surpluses of money which they want to invest overseas. Globally these funds control around $2.9 trillion and are growing rapidly.

Assets managed by sovereign wealth funds, 2008, $ billions

Country	Fund	Assets
UAE	Abu Dhabi Investment Authority	875
Singapore	Gov. of Sing. Invest. Corp. (GIC)	330
Norway	Government Pension Fund - Global	322
Saudi Arabia	Saudi Arabian Monet. Auth.	300
Kuwait	Kuwait Invest. Auth	250
China	China Investment Corporation	200
Russia	Stab. Fund of the Russian Fed.	127
Singapore	Temasek Holdings	108
Libya	Reserve Fund	50
Qatar	Qatar Investment Authority, 2000	40
Others		268
Total		**2,870**

Source: OECD (2008), using estimates by Deutsche Bank

attract much attention, operating quietly and often in secrecy. This was largely because most were controlled by regimes friendly to the West. Indeed generally their investments were welcomed since they were recycling money back to the oil purchasers who were only too pleased to see their money return. But attitudes started to change when Russia established its stabilization fund in 2003 and China established its Investment Corporation in 2007. These upstarts are less likely to play by the rules of Western countries and have upset some of the older funds – which have complained to the head of the Chinese fund about the unwelcome attention it has drawn to their business.

Where do they invest their money? They put much of it into various banks and funds. China, for example, has invested in the private equity company Blackstone, Singapore owns chunks of both Barclays Bank and the Swiss bank UBS. Abu Dhabi owns part of Citigroup. Skeptics may note that these have not proved very sound investments. The China Investment Corporation's $3 billion investment in Blackstone was followed by a collapse in its share price and the Corporation suffered similar losses as a result of buying $5 billion-worth of shares of the investment bank Morgan Stanley. Indeed in 2008, with bank share prices halving, some sovereign wealth funds earned a reputation as 'dumb money'.

A number of Western countries are worried, however, that these funds will get smarter and will start to buy up key strategic assets or use their financial muscle to exert political influence on Western companies and governments. The European Commission has introduced a code which requires sovereign wealth funds to declare where the money comes from and what they are doing with it, and to promise to avoid using investments for political purposes. Given the governments involved, however, this is being rather optimistic.[26]

Capital casinos

In fact one fund makes no secret of its political agenda. The Norwegian fund, for example, is known for its ethical stance. A panel of experts evaluates the 7,000 so companies it holds shares in and recommends disinvestment if required. One of its most notable decisions was to pull out of Wal-Mart, because of the company's poor record on labor rights in developing countries through the use of exploitative sub-contractors.

Another spin of the wheel

The capitalist system has thus devised ever more sophisticated ways of linking savers and borrowers – and allowing each to profit from the other. All involve some risk, and financial systems are inherently unstable and vulnerable to external events and changes in mood and opinion. With appropriate regulation these risks are usually manageable at the national level. But nowadays all financial systems are linked with those in other countries. The next chapter explores this mutual dependence by looking more closely at systems of international exchange.

1 Bank of England, 2008. *The inflation calculator*. www.bankofengland. co.uk 2 Shlomo Reifman & Samantha N Wong, 2005, *America's Largest Private Companies*. www.forbes.com/2005/11/09/largest-private-companies_05private_land.html 3 Milmo, C 2004. 'Ikea founder overtakes Bill Gates in the wealth stakes. (And he assembled it all himself)'. London, *The Independent*, 6 April. 4 EIU, 2008. *Financial Centres, US*, London, Economist Intelligence Unit. 5 *The Economist*, 2001. 'A penny in whose pocket?', in The Economist, 24 May. 6 *The Economist*, 2008. 'Legal advice', in The Economist, 21 August. 7 Bishop, M, *Essential Economics*, London, Profile Books. 8 EIU, *Financial Centres, UK*. London, Economist Intelligence Unit. 9 *The Economist*, 2003. 'The law of averages', in The Economist, 3 July. 10 *The Economist*, 2008. 'Private investigations', in The Economist, 3 July. 11 *Forbes, 2008. 400 richest people in America, Forbes* online. www.forbes.com 12 Levinson, M. 2006. *Guide to Financial Markets*, London, Profile Books. 13 EIU, 2008. *Financial Centres, Canada*, London, Economist Intelligence Unit. 14 EIU, 2008. *Financial Centres, Canada*, London, Economist Intelligence Unit. 15 *The Economist*, 2008. 'Clare and present danger', in The Economist, 6 November. 16 US Treasury, 2008. www.treasurydirect.gov/govt/resources/faq/faq_publicdebt. htm#DebtOwner 17 EIU, 2008, 2007. *Australia, country profile*. London, Economist Intelligence Unit. 18 ONS, 2008. Office of National Statistics.

www.statistics.gov.uk **19** Clark, A, 2008. 'How to set up a hedge fund', in *The Guardian*, 6 August. **20** *The Economist*, 2008. 'The incredible shrinking funds', in *The Economist*, 25 October. **21** *The Economist*, 2008. 'Phantom menace', in *The Economist*, 14 August. **22** Maher, S. 2008. The Hedge Fund Hustle, blog at *Seeking Alpha*, posted on: 15 August. **23** Farrell D and S Lund. 2007. 'The world's new financial power brokers', in *McKinsey Quarterly*: The Online Journal of McKinsey & Co. www.mckinseyquarterly.com **24** Morris, C. 2008. *The Trillion Dollar Meltdown*, New York, Public Affairs. **25** Blundell-Wignall, A Yu-Wei Hu and J Yermo. 'Sovereign Wealth and Pension Fund Issues', in *Financial Market Trends*, Paris, OECD 2008. **26** Halliday, F. 2008. 'Sovereign Wealth Funds: power vs principle'. Opendemocracy.net. Created 5 March.

5 Coping with currency

In a globalized world, the strength or weakness of a national economy should be reflected in the value of its currency. But as well as responding to economic signals, currencies can also swing wildly in value when they come under speculative attack. In self defense, some countries have come together to share a currency. Others throw in the towel and adopt the money of another country, often the US dollar.

IN AN ERA of globalization, we are well aware of how countries have become more financially interdependent. A crisis of confidence in New York will inevitably be followed by jitters in London, Frankfurt, Hong Kong and Tokyo – and will be reflected in fluttering share prices or stuttering demand for commodities or consumer goods. One of the most direct indicators of the shifting balance of financial power is expressed through currency exchange rates.

The earliest international traders did not worry too much about exchange rates. Either they bartered with their trading partners – exchanging manufactured trinkets, perhaps, for spices or furs or exotic foreign silks. Or they could use a universal medium of exchange such as gold or silver. But as trading activity increased, so too did the use of national currencies. Traders arriving in fifth-century Athens, for example, would have to get local currencies from moneychangers who would set up their tables in the market place. In modern Greek the word *trapeza* means both a table and a bank.[1] Even when both currencies used gold coins, traders generally felt more comfortable working with local currency since they might not trust strange foreign coins and were uncertain of their gold content.

One and a half millennia later the international flow of currencies has not just become vastly greater but also increasingly frenzied. In 2007, the world's foreign exchange markets bought and sold on average $3.2 trillion dollars-worth every day.[2] You might think this just reflected the need to buy and sell goods across international frontiers, but in fact it is around 30 times greater than the flow of international trade.

The value of currencies

What determines the relationship between one currency and another? What is one pound, or one dollar, or one rupee actually worth? Ultimately what matters is what can be bought. To assess their comparative values, you might look therefore at what it costs to buy the same commodity or item in different countries. This is not as simple as you might think since across the world people buy different things. Even the most basic foods have many grades. Rice, for example, has around 7,000 varieties – basmati rice in India, for example, or Jasmine rice in Thailand. So assessing currencies according to how much rice they will buy in each country could lead you astray.

What is needed therefore is something for which there is a clear international standard. *The Economist* magazine has a not entirely serious, but instructive, point of homogenized reference – the McDonalds Big Mac, an item produced to the same relentless recipe in around 120 countries. If you know, for example, that in the US the Big Mac costs $3.57 and that in Argentina it costs 11 pesos, you might guess that the exchange rate in terms of pesos to the dollar is 11 divided by 3.57 which would make it around three. Assessing currencies in this way is referred to as using 'purchasing power parity' (PPP). In fact for the Argentinean peso the value in the foreign exchange markets has been similar to that suggested by the Big Mac: in July 2008 the rate was 3.02 pesos to the dollar.[3] There has also been a reasonable correspondence for other currencies, such as Peru's new sol or the Australian dollar (see graphic 'Burgernomics').

Coping with currency

'Burgernomics'

To assess the comparative values of currencies, you might look at what it costs to buy the same thing in different countries. *The Economist* magazine has an instructive point of homogenized reference – the McDonalds Big Mac, produced to the same formula in around 120 countries. If you know, for example, that in the US a Big Mac costs $3.57 and that in Argentina it costs 11 pesos, you might guess that the exchange rate in terms of pesos to the dollar is 11 divided by 3.57 which would make it around three – and in July 2008 the rate was 3.02 pesos to the dollar.

Big Mac index, 2008

	Big Mac price in local currency	Implied exchange rate	Market exchange rate
United States	$3.57	–	–
Argentina	Peso 11.0	3.08	3.02
Australia	A$3.45	0.97	1.00
Britain	£2.29	1.56	2.00
Canada	C$4.09	1.15	1.00
Chile	Peso 1,550	434	494
China	Yuan 12.5	3.50	6.83
Indonesia	Rupiah 18,700	5,238	9,152
Japan	Yen 260	78.4	106.8
Malaysia	Ringgit 5.50	1.54	3.2
Mexico	Peso 320	8.55	10.2
New Zealand	NZ$4,90	1.37	1.32
Norway	Kroner 40.00	11.2	5.08
Pakistan	Rupee 140.00	39.22	70.90
Peru	New Sol.50	2.66	2.84
Philippines	Peso 87.00	24.37	44.49
Russia	Ruble 59.0	16.5	23.2
Singapore	S$3.95	1.11	1.35
Slovakia	Koruna 77.00	21.57	19.13
South Africa	Rand 16.9	4.75	7.56
Sri Lanka	Rupee 210.00	58.82	107.55
Sweden	SKr 38.00	10.6	5.86
Switzerland	SFr 6.50	1.82	1.02
Taiwan	NT$75.0	21.0	30.4
Thailand	Baht 62.0	17.4	33.4
Turkey	Lire 5.15	1.44	1.19
Uruguay	Peso 61.00	17.09	19.15

Source: *Economist*, 2008

For other currencies, however, the two assessments are some distance apart: in the case of the Norwegian kroner, for example, by a factor of two. This might suggest that there is something wrong with the Big Mac index – a fundamental flaw in *The Economist*'s 'burgernomics'. One factor is that the price of the burger will depend not only on its ingredients, which are mostly traded internationally, but also on things for which prices are set locally such as wage costs or rents which are likely to be quite different in New York, or Oslo or Kolkata. The other possibility is that the markets are pricing currencies on things other than their local purchasing power.

Earn in Denmark, spend in Mexico

The OECD has calculated for many countries how much it would cost in their own currency to buy the same basket of goods in many other countries at prevailing exchange rates.* The results are shown here for Australian dollars. The same basket of goods that would cost A$100 in Australia would cost only A$61 in Mexico but A$141 in Denmark. This shows how the relative value of currencies is set only partially by what they will buy. The cost of living can vary greatly between one country and another.

*OECD, 2008. *Purchasing power parities.* www.oecd.org/dataoecd/48/18/18598721.pdf

Comparative price levels around the world in Australian dollars

Source: OECD, 2008

Coping with currency

A more sophisticated approach extends the purchasing power parity method beyond Big Macs to include a more extensive 'basket' of goods. This is used as the basis of international statistics comparing the cost of living between different countries (see graphic *Earn in Denmark, spend in Mexico*).

In practice, currency dealers are often less interested in the fundamentals of what currencies are really worth and more interested how exchange rates are likely to change today or tomorrow. In this case, it is simpler to consider currency prices in terms of supply and demand. The demand for dollars will go up if people in the UK, for example, need dollars to buy US goods, or invest in US companies, or buy US treasury bonds. Rising demand for these will push up the value of the dollar. On the other hand if consumers or companies in the US want to import more from Europe or Asia, they will have to exchange their dollars for other currencies, and this will tend to push the value of the dollar down. Similar trade and investment takes place across over one hundred countries – setting market prices for currencies based on supply and demand.

In addition, you can get a price not just for selling euros or rupees now but also for doing so in three months' time, or up to one year. Just as you can buy futures in wheat or coffee, so you can buy futures in currencies. This is useful for exporters who will be paid for their goods in a foreign currency and want to 'lock in' their income.

Governments intervene

A further consideration is the activity of governments. Generally speaking, individuals and companies in the UK, for example, will not want to hold dollars. If they do not spend them on buying goods from the US or invest in the US they will sell the dollars for pounds. The British government, however, via the Bank of England, may well want to keep stocks of foreign currencies to add to its reserves of dollars or yen or euros. It uses these reserves for various purposes. One is to buffer short-term fluctuations in trade or investment – as exports or imports go up and down from month to month the Bank will have the flexibility to add to or draw from its currency reserves to avoid unnecessary fluctuations in exchange rates.

Governments can also deploy their foreign currency reserves to influence exchange rates. The Bank of England, for example, might consider that the pound is temporarily undervalued – which would make imports more expensive than necessary and increase inflation. If it has sufficient reserves of dollars or other currencies it can use these to buy pounds – which should increase the demand for pounds and thus push the exchange rate up.

In addition, governments can influence exchange rates by altering interest rates. Perhaps the British government is worried about inflation so it wants to cut the money supply by reducing bank borrowing. In this case it could raise the interest rate. A Canadian investor spotting that interest rates are higher in London than Toronto may then be tempted to change their Canadian dollars to pounds and deposit them in British banks. But he or she would also have to take into account not just differences in interest rates between Canada and the UK but also in the rates of inflation. There is little point in moving funds into the UK for a few percentage points difference in the interest rates if the value of your funds, which are now in pounds, is rapidly eroded by inflation. Moving currencies around is a tricky business.

Enter the speculators
Exchange rates are thus affected by the costs of goods in different countries and by interest and inflation rates – and by the pressures of supply and demand resulting

from international trade. But exchange rates fluctuate much more rapidly than these basic factors would warrant, and the volume of international currencies bought and sold is vastly greater than the value of international trade. This suggests that something else is at work, encouraging people to move money in and out of currencies on a daily basis. In fact volatility in the currency markets is largely the result of speculation.

Currency traders do try to make their decisions based on events in the real world. So they always wait eagerly for data on imports and exports because these can signal potential changes in currency values. If Indonesian exports fall and imports rise, then supply and demand is likely to push down the value of the Indonesian rupiah. But traders can also amplify these trends by their own actions. Any trader who starts selling rupiah on the basis of a rise in Indonesian food imports will depress the demand for rupiah still further. Much of the activity in the foreign exchange markets is driven not just by real events but by expectations. All of this results in frenzied activity, especially in London, the location for around one third of foreign exchange trading – $1.4 trillion worth per day.

The costs of trading are low, as little as 0.002 per cent on each deal, and screen-based transactions are completed in milliseconds.[4] This allows traders to respond on the slightest whim, or the guess of a change in interest rates or inflation figures, shifting around millions of dollars at a time. Foreign exchange trading is also hugely profitable. In the US, for example, for the big commercial banks foreign exchange dealing accounts for around half their profits.[5]

When does currency trading venture into speculation? Partly this is a matter of scale. Traders may be dealing in millions of dollars at a time, but high-rolling speculators, such as George Soros, have also manipulated currency markets and that takes serious money.

Exchange rate systems

Nowadays, partly as a result of this intensive trading, the rates for most of the world's major currencies fluctuate daily – a far cry from the more sedate era when currencies scarcely moved since most of them were yoked together via the 'gold standard'. This standard emerged around the middle of the 19th century when the central banks of most Western countries behaved in a highly disciplined fashion, only issuing new paper currency that corresponded to the same amounts of gold in their vaults. So in principle anyone with a banknote could exchange this for the value in gold. The Bank of England embraced the gold standard in 1821, followed by Australia and Canada and later by Germany, Scandinavia, Holland, Belgium, Switzerland, France and the United States. Later the system spread to Asia, including Japan, the Straits Settlements, India and the Philippines. By 1910 most nations were on the gold standard.

At the beginning of the 20th century, for example, £1 was fixed at 22 ounces of gold, and $1 at 4.5 ounces. Divide one weight by the other and you get a fixed exchange rate in which £1 was worth $4.86 – with corresponding ratios for other currencies.[6] For foreign exchange this offered a system that was adjusted by flows of gold. If France successfully exported more wine to Germany, and accumulated deutschmarks, it could exchange these for gold with the Bundesbank. Imbalances were therefore resolved by transfers of gold into and out of countries.

The gold standard broke down temporarily from 1914 with the outbreak of the First World War. As a result of paying for troops and equipment, the warring countries soon exhausted their supplies of gold and suspended the promise to exchange banknotes for gold. For the losing country, Germany, this would eventually lead to the collapse of its currency. Faced with demands for reparations from the victors in the conflict, the German government printed a large number of banknotes. Such was the pace of inflation that a single egg was eventually priced at four billion deutschmarks. The current world record for hyper-inflation, however, was established in this era by Hungary. Following rampant inflation, the national currency, the pengo, was soon expressed in 'bilpengos', billions of pengos, and the central bank finally issued a 100 million bilpengo note that had to find room for 18 zeros.[7]

After the First World War most countries returned to the gold standard. While this offered some stability it did so at a heavy cost. Countries with imbalances that were losing gold would see their supply of money dwindle. With less money around, prices would fall – deflation – and the economy would go into recession. Since consumers could not afford imports, the country's foreign exchange accounts would be wrenched back into balance. The economy might be stable again, but at a lower level, with many people unemployed.

The Bretton Woods system

After the Second World War a conference at Bretton Woods in New Hampshire, which also saw the establishment of the World Bank and the International Monetary Fund (IMF), introduced a somewhat more flexible system. This effectively meant that the US fixed the dollar to gold, at $35 per ounce, and other countries fixed their currencies to the dollar at a 'par' value. This 'Gold Exchange System' required central banks to buy and sell their currencies so as to keep them within 1 per cent of the 'par' value. This system was not as rigid as the earlier gold standard since countries suffering persistent balance of payments problems could under certain circumstances either devalue their currencies to a lower exchange rate, or borrow gold or foreign exchange from the IMF to tide them over. Within this system, the British pound was steadily devalued, from

$4.03 in 1944, to $2.80 in 1949, to $2.40 in 1967. The British government was also to suffer in 1976 the ignominy of going 'cap in hand' to the IMF for a loan of $2.3 billion.

Eventually the Bretton Woods exchange system also broke down, and for an all-too-familiar reason: war. The US came off this fixed standard in 1971 because financing the war in Vietnam was draining its gold reserves. Subsequently other developed countries decided that their countries could 'float' against the dollar, much as they do today. But floating does not suit all countries. Those with more fragile monetary systems decided not to risk instability. Instead they preferred to fix, or 'peg' their currency to another one, commonly the US dollar. So as the dollar went up and down in a more controlled fashion their currency would follow suit. As an extension of this system, governments can also establish a 'currency board' – a new monetary authority which takes over one of the central bank's functions, that of issuing the national currency. A currency board can only issue new banknotes if it has received corresponding new supplies of foreign exchange.

The main problem with any fixed rate system is that a degree of stability is obtained only at the price of a loss of government control over monetary policy. Governments and central banks value the flexibility offered by manipulating interest rates. They may want to increase interest rates to control inflation, for example, or reduce them if they are faced with high unemployment and want to stimulate economic activity. But if they have a fixed or pegged rate, then in order to keep the currency at this rate they have to adjust the interest rate – raising it to attract foreign capital, for example, if the exchange rate is under pressure. If governments use interest rates primarily to support the currency they lose the freedom to adjust rates in accordance with the need to control inflation or increase employment.

Coping with currency

Currency crises

There is a limit to which governments can defend their exchange rates. If the rates get too far out of line with a country's economic reality then the illusionary security of fixed rates can be followed by an implosion. This happened in 1997 in the Asian financial crisis that started in Thailand. While the crisis had multiple causes in different countries, currency pegs played their part.

In Thailand during the early 1990s, the currency – the baht – was pegged at 25 to the dollar. Meanwhile in the dollar's home, the United States, interest rates were very low. Thai companies and individuals took advantage of these circumstances to borrow hefty sums in dollars, feeling confident that they would be able to earn enough baht to pay off their dollar debts by exchanging them at the bargain rate of 25 to the dollar. The result was an explosion of speculative investment, particularly in flashy skyscrapers in Bangkok. All of this was also encouraged by the Asian economic 'miracle', based on rapidly rising exports of electronic and other goods.

Then the deals started to unravel. First, demand for Thailand's exports started to slow, putting pressure on the baht. Second, the US government became worried about inflation so increased its interest rates – making it more difficult for Thai borrowers to service their loans. With the writing on the wall, speculators and investors started to lose faith that Thailand would defend the baht and capital started to flee. This exacerbated the problem, eventually forcing the government to let the baht float, and in 1998 it duly soared to 56 to the dollar. People who had taken out dollar loans now had to earn more than twice as many baht to service them; many were forced into bankruptcy – leaving the Bangkok skyline in suspended animation with half-finished buildings and idle cranes. The crisis then spread to other countries such as Indonesia, and even to stronger economies,

George Soros, the man who broke the Bank of England

In 1979 before the introduction of the euro, the European Community devised the 'Exchange Rate Mechanism'. The aim was to stabilize currencies by allowing them to float within a limited range or 'band'. When the currency moved outside the band the central bank had to adjust interest rates or buy or sell its currency to bring the exchange rate back into line. The UK joined the Exchange Rate Mechanism in 1990 but set an ambitiously high rate. By 1992, the pound was slipping out of its band – forcing the British government to take ever more desperate measures, raising interest rates and buying pounds.

The currency speculators sniffed an impending disaster. The arch speculator was George Soros, then heading a hedge fund, the Quantum Fund. He did not believe that the British government could sustain its defense and started to bet against the pound by selling 'futures' – contracts to provide sterling in three or six months. Anticipating devaluation he bought £6 billion. The showdown came on 'Black Wednesday', 16 September 1992. The British government frantically raised the base interest rate first to 10 per cent then to 12 per cent and finally to a bizarre 15 per cent. Finally, and after spending £3.2 billion in a vain effort to prop up the pound, the authorities threw in the towel and conceded to the speculators, letting the pound float down. When the pound suddenly sank, Soros could provide his promised pounds at a rate far cheaper than he had bought them, walking away with around $1 billion in profit, and an enduring reputation as the 'man who broke the Bank of England'.

including the Republic of Korea.

But exchange rate disasters do not happen only in developing countries. In 1997 the British government provided an iconic example of how not to control floating exchange rates – and lost over £3 billion in the process (see box *George Soros*).

Nevertheless governments and central banks still try to manage exchange rates to some extent. They can do this simply by announcements or giving hints about future inflation data or possibilities of changes in interest rates, or actual changes. Or they may buy or sell currencies. Ultimately, however, they cannot affect long-term fundamental rates, since even national currency reserves are dwarfed by the volumes traded daily in the currency markets.

Coping with currency

Monetary unions

For countries that trade extensively with each other it would be much more convenient to avoid the hassle of fluctuating exchange rate by sharing a common currency. The United States could be considered a monetary union since it uses a single currency across 50 very different states. In the past such unions have been imposed by force by colonial powers. But more recently countries have entered into unions voluntarily. The most notable case is that of the European Union where one currency, the euro, is used by 15 states. The euro and its interest rate are controlled by an independent body based in Frankfurt, the European Central Bank (ECB). The 15 national central-bank governors go to Frankfurt twice a month to rubber-stamp decisions taken by the ECB's executive board.

The main argument in favor of a monetary union is that it creates a more stable environment. Consumers can compare prices in different countries. Companies do not have to worry that changes in exchange rates will affect their profits. And governments, particularly of smaller countries, do not have to worry about currency speculators ganging up on them. The main disadvantage is the 'one-size-fit-all' approach. When they sign up for the euro, for example, each country has to accept a 'Stability and Growth Pact', agreeing on some common economic policies, in particular not running large budget deficits. But this can create severe constraints.

All countries go through economic cycles, with periods of higher growth and low unemployment, followed by periods of lower growth and higher unemployment. It is very unlikely that these cycles will coincide across member countries – which means that at any time some will have the wrong monetary policies. A country with high unemployment, for example, might want to have lower interest rates to stimulate growth, while one with higher growth might want a higher interest rate to dampen down inflation. The US, as a monetary union between states, may appear to have a similar problem, but in this case there can be some equalization since workers can easily move from a depressed state to a faster growing one. In principle Europeans have the same flexibility, but in practice workers are more reluctant to relocate. So far Portugal, Italy, Greece and Spain have been out of sync with France and Germany, as their booms in the early 2000s were followed by the inevitable busts, tempting the European Central Bank to lower interest rates at that time to help them out.[8]

The euro is by no means the only monetary union. A number of African countries, mostly former French colonies, have unions in West Africa and Central Africa that share a 'CFA franc', while others in the Pacific share a 'CFP franc'. In the Caribbean a group of smaller islands share the East Caribbean dollar.

Dollarization

In modern monetary unions, countries enter into voluntary agreements through which they share the responsibility for monetary management. Some countries, however, have submitted to much more one-sided arrangements – abandoning their own currency and simply adopting that of a more powerful economy. Panama, for example, has long lived under the shadow of the United States. Although independent since 1903 it only gained control over its most valuable asset, the canal, in 1999. Officially it has its own currency, the balboa, but issues this only in coins, and for most purposes uses the US dollar. US colonization also resulted in a legacy use of the dollar in other now independent states such as the Federated States of Micronesia.

Dollarization often happens unofficially during warfare or at a time of economic crisis that causes people to lose confidence in their own currency. When for example Timor-Leste gained its independence in 1999, it wanted to get rid of the Indonesian rupiah as soon as possible, and so adopted the US dollar. Although it now issues its own coins, centavos, which are equivalent to US cents, Timor-Leste still uses dollar bills.

Other countries have also collapsed into the dollar's embrace. In 2001 El Salvador introduced a Monetary Integration Law which established a dual currency system, using both the colón and the dollar which were fixed at the same value. In practice, for nearly all commercial transactions people use dollars. The most contentious case, however, was in Ecuador. In 1999, Ecuador was in dire economic straits and had to default on government bonds. The following year, President Jamil Mahoud proposed to replace the national currency, the sucre, with the dollar. This outraged trade unions and Amerindian groups who marched in protest on the capital. The army stepped in and replaced Mahoud with his vice-president Gustavo Noboa – who pressed on with dollarization anyway.

Countries that want to adopt another country's currency do not have to use the dollar. A number of European microstates such as Montenegro use the euro. The Vatican too uses the euro though it is also allowed to produce a limited number of its own euro coins. In the Pacific, some of the small island states use the currencies of their larger neighbors. The Cook Islands, for example, uses the New Zealand dollar and Kiribati and Nauru use the Australian dollar.

Why would any state want to give up the right to control its own currency? In some cases, it is because politicians have little faith in the monetary authorities, and fear that future governments that want to get out of an economic hole will be tempted to print money and thus trigger hyperinflation. Dollarization removes this risk and offers comfort to international investors who will always know the dollar value of their investments. Dollarization also protects the country from attacks by currency speculators and helps exporters engage more easily in international trade.

But there are heavy costs. One is the loss of 'seignorage'. This refers to the income that the government gets when it manufactures coins and notes that have a much higher value than their production cost, and is thus able to spend the difference. But the most serious disadvantage is a mirror image of one of the advantages. The government has fewer opportunities to make bad decisions but is also less able to make good ones – such as adjusting interest rates to boost employment. The central bank also has less freedom to support banks that get into difficulties. It might be able to lend some of its dollars, but without the flexibility to print money it cannot really serve as the 'lender of last resort'.

Foreign exchange reserves

Though few countries have resorted to dollarization, all must keep substantial quantities of dollars in their reserves. Central banks have to hold foreign currency reserves to act as a buffer in case of temporary trade or other deficits. They can also use them to buy the national currency if they want to push up the exchange rate so as to make imports cheaper. Globally, foreign exchange reserves have been rising steeply. At the beginning of 2008, the reserves held by all countries came to $6.8 trillion. Of the reserves whose currency is known, around 60 per cent were held in US dollars and most of the rest in euros. In the past, the pound sterling used to be one of the world's major reserve currencies but now accounts for only around 2 per cent.[9]

In 2008 central banks outside the US were holding around $4 trillion. Generally they will have built up these reserves by saving rather than spending the dollars they have acquired by trading with the United States, or by buying foreign currency in the foreign exchange markets. Some of this is in dollar bills, but most will be in the form of US Treasury bonds or deposits in US banks.

Coping with currency

When other countries hold onto dollars this is effectively a huge gift to the United States. It is as though the US Treasury has been able to write $4 trillion in checks that no-one has ever cashed. This has enabled the US to embark on a long consumer boom and run a persistent trade deficit since 1975, reaching a record $817 billion by 2006. This all adds up. Divide $4 trillion by the US population and you find that each citizen on average now owes the rest of the world around $13,000. Moreover, that only takes into account intergovernmental debt; even more US Treasury bonds are held by foreign corporations and individuals.

A number of countries have been able to boost their reserves substantially in recent years. Oil and gas exporters, including Russia, have benefited from periods of booming commodity prices. But the most striking increases have been in Asia (see graphic *Asian reserves rise*). Some of this has come from success in manufactured exports. China, for example, by 2007

Asian reserves rise

By the end of 2009 Asia as a whole could have $5.1 trillion in reserves. This shift of reserves to the region is one of the most remarkable transfers of global wealth ever.

International reserves in Asia ($ billions)

	2003	2007	2008 (est)	2009 (est)
China	403	1,499	1,940	2,417
Hong Kong	118	146	151	149
India	107	284	344	414
Indonesia	36	56	55	53
Japan	674	983	1,076	1,134
Korea	155	265	271	271
Malaysia	45	103	106	100
Philippines	17	33	34	34
Singapore	96	162	183	202
Taiwan	207	272	274	276
Thailand	42	81	97	102

Source: Berthelsen, 2008

---

had accumulated around $1.5 trillion in reserves. But other Asian countries have together assembled more than that, and by the end of 2009 Asia as a whole could have $5.1 trillion.[10]

This shift of reserves to Asia is one of the most remarkable transfers of global wealth in history. Following the 1997 financial crisis, Asian countries were understandably keen to avoid any repeat of that disaster and resolutely accumulated reserves as a kind of insurance policy. They could do this because over the past 10 years the industrialized countries have been investing in Asia to take advantage of low labor costs and the prospect of new markets. Asian countries responded by selling manufactured goods to the West for foreign currency. Rather than spending this, however, they recycled a significant part of the proceeds into US Treasury and government bonds and other investments. In some cases, they have done this through central banks; in others through sovereign wealth funds. The net result is that they now have reserves far beyond what they need for safety.

You might think this is dangerous. What happens if China starts to sell some of its dollar bonds? US consumers will suffer from a dollar collapse. No more cheap TVs or computers. But the Asian countries would need to think twice before dumping their dollars. If international markets believe that China is going to sell its dollars, the dollar would nosedive and the value of Asia's hard-earned assets would also sink. This is rather like the relationship between a bank and its customers. If you borrow a small amount from the bank, the bank owns you. If you borrow a huge amount, then you 'own' the bank which will be terrified that you will default.

Nevertheless, many people in Asia are becoming restless about the use of their funds to prop up the US economy and have suggested better uses for the money. One possibility is to invest in infrastructure.

Coping with currency

Across Asia, roads, railways, energy plants, airports, sea ports, telecommunications grids and bridges are creaking under the strain of economic growth. It has been estimated that from 2006 to 2010 the developing countries in Asia and the Pacific need to invest $228 billion annually. One suggestion for putting this into practice is to establish an Asian Investment Bank that could take some of the reserves languishing at low interest rates in the US and instead disperse them across the region. So far, however, such concerted action has been very limited.[11]

For many other developing countries, however, the problem is not too much foreign exchange but too little. Facing economic crises and spiraling international debt, they have been pushed into the arms of Washington's 'ugly sisters', the IMF and the World Bank – which are the focus of the next chapter.

1 Eagleton, C and Williams, J. 2007. *Money: a history, London*, British Museum Press. **2** BIS, 2008. *Triennial Central Bank Survey. Foreign exchange and derivatives market activity in 2007*. Basel, Bank for International Settlements. **3** *The Economist*, 2008. "Sandwiched", in *The Economist*, 24 July. **4** EIU 2008, *Financial Centres, UK*. London, Economist Intelligence Unit. **5** Valdez, S. 2007. *An Introduction to Global Financial Markets*, Basingstoke, Palgrave Macmillan. **6** Levinson, M. 2006. *Guide to financial markets*, London, Profile. **7** Starck, J. 2005. 'Feels like a million bucks'. www.coinworld.com/news/090505/bw_0905.asp **8** *The Economist*, 2008. "A decade in the sun" in *The Economist*, 5 June. **9** IMF, 2008. Currency Composition of Official Foreign Exchange Reserves (COFER) www.imf.org/external/np/sta/cofer/eng/index.htm **10** Berthelsen, John. 2008. 'Asia Ponders Its Astounding Foreign Exchange Reserves', www.asiasentinel.com **11** UNESCAP, 2008. *Economic and Social Survey of Asia and the Pacific*, Bangkok, United Nations.

6 The ugly sisters

Until recently, most of the world's financial crises have been concentrated in developing countries which then had to resort to loans from the World Bank and the IMF. For these two institutions, emergencies such as the 'Third World Debt' crisis and the Asian financial crisis created welcome opportunities to push their own free-market ideologies, often with disastrous consequences.

THE RECENT CONVULSIONS in international finance have frequently drawn comparisons with the great Wall Street crash of the 1930s. This was famously an era when ruined capitalists were supposedly jumping out of windows. Not much sign of defenestration this time round, perhaps because many banks can rely on 'golden parachutes', and many of the fast-talking traders have already cushioned any falls with fat bonuses.

This time too the response of governments has been very different. In 2008 when faced with failing banks, George Bush's banker-friendly treasury secretary Hank Paulsen, a former chief executive officer of the investment bank Goldman Sachs, tried to cheer them up by loaning billions of dollars. In 1929 the policy of the then treasury secretary Andrew Mellon was very different – 'liquidate, liquidate, liquidate', as he sought to 'purge the rottenness out of the system'. Mellon might well have cleaned things up but his ideological purity is also thought to have plunged America into the Great Depression.

The experience of the 1930s so scarred the world's governments that when they were planning post-War War Two reconstruction they aimed to rebuild not just Europe's bomb-blasted cities but also the global financial architecture. As a consequence, under the influence of major figures, such as British economist John Maynard Keynes, governments all over the world were to become much more interventionist, regularly trying to stabilize economies and markets in the hope of achieving low inflation and low unemployment.

These debates culminated in July 1944 in a landmark event: the United Nations Monetary and Financial Conference, held at Bretton Woods in New Hampshire and attended by representatives from 45 countries. At that point, however, only two voices really mattered, those of the victorious allies, the US and the UK. Indeed, in many respects the Bretton Woods conference essentially formalized agreements already reached by these two countries. The outcome was two major institutions: the International Monetary Fund (IMF), and the International Bank for Reconstruction and Development (IBRD) which later became part of the World Bank. There was also a proposal for an International Trade Organization, though this was to emerge simply as a treaty, the General Agreement on Trade and Tariffs, and only took institutional form from 1995, as the World Trade Organization.

The International Monetary Fund

The IMF was designed to help counter the exchange rate anarchy of the interwar years and promote international monetary co-operation and stable exchange rates. Governments agreed to keep their currencies at an agreed fixed rate in relation to gold, which at the outset was around $35 per ounce. If the rate moved more that 1 per cent from its agreed 'par value' the central bank would intervene and buy or sell the currency as appropriate. If it wanted to change the par value it would need permission from the IMF.

Each country that joins the Fund pays a 'subscription' – one quarter of which has to be in gold or in a 'hard' convertible currency such as the US dollar or the Japanese yen. It can pay the rest in the national currency. The amount of the subscription varies according to the size of the economy and the extent of the country's international trade – to correspond roughly to its use of international currencies. Crucially, the size of the subscription also determines the country's influence. Unlike in the United Nations, which is based on one country, one vote, the voting power in the IMF depends ultimately on economic clout. As a result, the largest contributor, the US, has 17 per cent of the votes; next come Japan and Germany with 6 per cent; France and the UK with 5 per cent; and China, Russia and Saudi Arabia with 3 per cent.

When foreign exchange reserves became dangerously low, say down to two or three weeks of typical trading, any country in trouble could borrow from the IMF. The initial loan was easy. Each country was automatically entitled to the first part, or 'tranche', which corresponded to its own currency, no questions asked. It was also able to borrow a further three times as much as this, the 'upper tranches', in hard currency; but in this case it had to convince the IMF that it was taking appropriate measures to correct its balance of payments problems so that it would be able to repay within the agreed period, usually one to five years. This involved the government signing a 'letter of intent'.

At the outset not everyone was keen that the IMF should have this powerful role. The British delegation at Bretton Woods argued that members should have automatic borrowing rights based on fixed rules with no special conditions. The US delegation on the other hand wanted to be able to dictate to the borrowers so as to increase the likelihood that the funds would be repaid. There were also arguments about where the bureaucracy would be located. The British argued for New York, but the US wanted it in Washington, where it would fall under the gaze of the US Treasury. Inevitably, as the dominant power and largest contributor to the Fund, the US had its way on both counts.

Although the IMF was originally created to focus on exchange rates and the balances of payments, its role changed over the years, especially after the 1970s. One major event was in the UK in 1976 when, faced with a balance of payments crisis, the government had to subject itself to a visit from the IMF which resulted in cuts in public expenditure and agreements not to impose import controls – a humiliating experience that reinforced the determination of developed countries never to turn to the IMF except as the last of all possible resorts.

IMF loans

This was largely because of the conditions of IMF loans. Article IV of the IMF's articles of agreement commits members to orderly economic growth and financial stability. But it does not specify in detail how to achieve this. This is not surprising since any country can be subject to a huge number of pressures, from drops in the price of its main commodities like copper or sugar, to political unrest, to natural disasters. One option, for example, might be to increase tariffs to make imports more expensive, or to subsidize export industries so that goods sell better overseas, or to stop multinational companies sending their profits home. This, however, would not go down well in Washington. Instead the IMF usually issues a standard set of prescriptions, its 'conditionalities'. Over the years, regardless of the circumstances of the country that needs to borrow, these conditionalities evolved into a rigid template – stabilize, liberalize, privatize, and deregulate.[1]

Presumably the IMF functionaries actually believed that these free market solutions would do the trick. More often, however, they knew relatively little of the complexity of national political and economic circumstances, and on their flying visits to distressed countries would simply present their template. Borrowers would be told to abolish any import or foreign exchange controls, raise interest rates and cut public expenditure, and reduce food or fuel subsidies. The main strategy was to make people poorer so they would be unable to afford imports. At the same time the borrowing country had to open its doors to foreign investors. Finance ministers would nod dutifully at all this – though they were well aware that many of these measures were pointless or impossible to implement, and just assumed that they could take the money and subsequently renege on their promises.

The World Bank

At this point the story of the IMF has to be complemented with that of the World Bank. Although they started with fairly distinct roles, the two were later to overlap considerably, bracketed sometimes as the 'ugly sisters'. In fact at the Bretton Woods conference the World Bank was something of an afterthought, and even that had little to do with developing countries. The conference wanted the IMF to provide member countries with funds to tide them over temporary balance of payments problems, while it wanted the World Bank, through the International Bank for Reconstruction and Development (IBRD), to support post-war reconstruction by providing longer-term funds to governments for specific infrastructure projects, such as roads and power supplies. Through a second of its institutions, the International Finance Corporation, the World Bank would fund private-sector projects.

Like the IMF, the World Bank was to acquire some of its funds as capital from subscribing countries. But it would get most of its funds by selling World Bank bonds on Wall Street, using investment bankers such as Morgan Stanley. As a US government-backed body, the World Bank automatically gets a solid 'triple-A' rating, so can borrow at the lowest rates and then add between 0.5 and 0.7 percentage points before lending on to borrowers. This should still give its borrowers better rates than they could get themselves. The World

The ugly sisters

Bank uses the mark-up to cover its $1.5 billion operating expenses. By paying itself with the profits on loans, the World Bank has a considerable advantage over other international development agencies. It can pay high salaries to its 10,000 or so employees and devote large sums to gather vast quantities of data and analysis. However, because it wants to be sure that it will be repaid it regularly sends intrusive and judgmental missions to check not just on individual projects but also on a government's overall policies to make sure they are following the World Bank's economic prescriptions.

The World Bank also has cheaper lending 'windows'. This facility dates back to the 1950s and the onset of the Cold War when governments of the richer capitalist countries were looking for allies in the Third World who might otherwise fall into the Soviet camp. As US Secretary of State, John Foster Dulles, put it: 'It might be good banking to put South America through the wringer, but it will come out red.'[2] It would be better therefore to find ways of getting cheaper loans to developing countries. The solution in 1960 was to add a further institution to the World Bank group, the International Development Association. This would lend funds on softer terms than the IBRD – at lower rates of interest and over longer periods. Funds for the IDA would, however, come not from bond sales but from periodically replenished capital 'subscriptions' by the richer countries. The IDA would specifically lend to the poorest countries and consider investments other than infrastructure – initially looking at agricultural development, but later investing in health and education.

The World Bank is primarily a US-inspired institution. All its presidents have been US citizens and most have close Wall Street connections. The 2008 incumbent, Robert Zoellick, was formerly a managing director of Goldman Sachs. Not surprisingly, therefore, it has marshaled its intellectual and financial clout in ways that reflect US preoccupations.

The Washington Consensus

By the 1970s, it had become clear that most of the World Bank's activities were not making much of an impact on poverty, particularly in sub-Saharan Africa. The World Bank's economists concluded that these countries needed something more fundamental. Failure, they decided, was clearly the fault of the recipient governments which were pursuing erroneous economic policies and needed to buck up their ideas. They should wean themselves away from state intervention in their economies and open up to the private sector and to flows of international trade and investment.

To persuade Third World governments to move in this direction, the IMF and the World Bank engaged in a pincer movement. The two institutions had always been close, literally so since they occupy offices on opposite sides of 16th Street in Washington, linked by an underground passageway. To ensure that the poorest developing countries were aligned with their joint worldview the IMF would make short-term stabilization loans to tide them over immediate financial crises, while the World Bank would make longer term 'structural adjustment' loans, to enable them to reorient their economies along free market lines. These moves were given a further impulse by the arrival of the Thatcher administration in the UK in 1979 and the Reagan administration in the US in 1980. The fused ideology of the US administration and the two Bretton Woods organizations came to be known as the 'Washington Consensus'.

This basically involved abandoning any socialist principles and embracing free market capitalism and in particular free trade. Strangely, this did not match the route that most of the developed countries had themselves traveled a hundred years or so earlier. Nor did it mirror the successful experience of the rapidly growing Asian tigers, most of whom had taken care to build up their economies behind tariff walls which they only removed when their industries were strong enough to withstand, or preferably beat, international competition.

Not surprisingly, for countries that followed, or were obliged to follow, the prescriptions of free market fundamentalism, the results varied from disappointing to disastrous. Sub-Saharan Africa generally failed to respond and remained desperately poor, and Latin American countries that dutifully dismantled their state-led, populist, and protectionist systems were rewarded with lower per-capita GDP growth in the 1990s than in any of the previous three decades.

The 'Third World Debt' crisis

On the financial front, one of the key assumptions was that developing countries needed to open up to flows of international capital. This was partly just a question of dogma: free market good; government controls bad. But there were also more specific promises. One was that, just as water will flow downhill, capital should be allowed to flow from rich countries, which have a lot of it, to poor countries where few people have savings. In some countries foreign investment and public loans have indeed stimulated economic development and reduced poverty. But in many others it has just landed the recipient countries with huge debts.

In 2008, the world's 142 'emerging and developing countries' owed $2.7 trillion to rich country creditors and in that year alone paid them $514 billion in 'debt service', which refers to a combination of interest charges and repayment of capital. Some of this is 'commercial debt' which is owed to banks and private companies, but the poorest countries in particular owe large sums to the World Bank and regional banks, as well as to donor countries in the form of 'bilateral debt'. As a result, for every $1 the developing countries receive in aid, they have to pay $5 in debt service.[3]

Some of this debt is legitimate. Governments all over the world borrow money from banks or from international organizations, to invest in infrastructure or schools or health services, on the assumption that future economic growth will sufficiently boost government income so as to allow them to repay through higher tax revenues. But many had other things in mind, especially the corrupt dictatorial regimes that then squandered the funds or siphoned them into their own Swiss bank accounts. Even the more democratic countries were offered funds by reckless lenders to finance dubious projects.

The result by the 1980s was the 'Third World Debt Crisis'. This had deep roots. Some reached back to the onset of the Cold War, when Western countries sought to prop up anti-communist regimes, offering loans at less than market rates – often for projects which were unviable even with cheap finance. But lending expanded dramatically in the 1970s, particularly after the first OPEC-driven 'oil shock' of 1973. Nowadays the oil-rich sultanates in the Gulf invest their vast quantities of surplus dollars in developed countries via sovereign wealth funds. In the 1970s, however, many also deposited the dollars in Western banks which suddenly found themselves awash with funds. Seeking new borrowers, the banks headed for developing countries. As a result, between 1970 and 1980 the debt of developing countries shot up from $70 billion to $580 billion, around half of which was in Latin America, which by then found itself shelling out around one third of the value of its exports just for servicing the debt.[4]

By the early 1990s the wheels were starting to come off this reckless lending cycle. On the one hand interest rates tripled, increasing the cost of the debt; on the other hand the prices for developing countries' export commodities such as coffee or cotton collapsed. Many countries found themselves borrowing more and more just to pay the interest on existing debts. This did not concern the banks too much until in 1982 Mexico threatened the unthinkable – that it would renege on its debts – to the horror of the banks that had made the foolish loans. The problem had now become more serious; it affected not just poor countries but rich Western banks. A familiar scenario ensued. If the banks failed, the world financial system was at risk. With the support of the IMF the banks got together and organized a scheme which would enable the borrowers to 'reschedule' their debts, paying them off over longer periods.

The Baker plan

A number of plans were put forward, of which the most durable came in 1989 from the then US treasury secretary, Nicholas Baker. Some of this involved exchanging the old bank loans for shiny new 'Brady bonds'. Banks would convert the loans into bonds which the US would help guarantee – and which could be sold on international bond markets. This helped defuse the immediate crisis for countries like Brazil and Mexico – whose debts had thus become tradable. Subsequently, many of these bonds were 'retired' – that is purchased back by the borrowing countries. The principles underlying the Brady bonds subsequently contributed to a thriving industry in bonds from 'emerging markets'.

For many of the poorer countries in Africa, however, it was clear that their debt, even as bonds, would be of little interest to the international markets. The World Bank and other agencies therefore lent them more money so they could pay off their old debts – transforming commercial debt not into bonds but into loans from international organizations: 'multilateral' debt. This of course did not solve the fundamental problem that many of these debts, commercial or multilateral, were simply unpayable – an issue highlighted by a coalition of NGOs that came together in 1996 as 'Jubilee 2000', calling for these debts to be cancelled.

Initiatives for the poorest countries

By 1992, the debts of the 33 most indebted low-income countries had soared to over six times their annual exports. Faced with rising public anger and the harsh reality that the poorest countries were servicing less than half their debts, the World Bank and the IMF devised the Heavily Indebted Poor Country (HIPC) initiative. The aim of the HIPC was to reduce the debts of the 40 poorest indebted countries, with an annual per capita income of around $900 or less, to a 'sustainable' level. Countries signing up to the HIPC get some immediate relief on debt repayment. But there are strings attached. Reasonably, these countries are required to show they are taking action to fight poverty. Less reasonably they also have to cut public spending, with dire effects for such services as education and health. They are also required to privatize public utilities for water or electricity, while also cutting tariff barriers to expose farmers and other small producers to the vagaries of international trade.

By 2005, it was clear that the HIPC was not going far enough and international activists, through campaigns such as 'Make Poverty History', put pressure on the G8 governments meeting at Gleneagles in Scotland to do more. The result was the 2006 Multilateral Debt Relief Initiative (MDRI). Previously, under the HIPC, enough debt would be written off to bring total debt down to a 'sustainable' level, which is taken to be one and a half times the value of export earnings. Now under the MDRI they would get more of their debt written off.

The HIPC and MDRI refer to debts to multilateral organizations and regional banks. But some countries also owe money to other countries – 'bilateral' debt. Some of this will have been accumulated through decades of aid, but around one third of bilateral debt has resulted from 'export credit guarantees'. Here, the rich countries have promised their own exporters that if the buyers in poor countries do not pay up, then the donor government will do so instead. Very generous you might think, and the exporters are doubtless grateful. But in fact the bills are paid by counting them as aid and adding these sums to the bilateral debt.

Periodically the world's bilateral creditors meet in Paris to negotiate with countries that are struggling to make their payments. At this 'Paris Club' they often reschedule the debt to give countries longer to pay, though they may also cancel the debt of the poorest countries that have jumped all the HIPC hurdles. Since 1996 the HIPC has cancelled more than $45 billion for 23 countries, while in 2007 the MDRI cancelled around $42 billion for 25 countries. Around two-thirds of this debt relief is earmarked for health and education. Debt relief has proved particularly valuable for a number of African countries.

In addition to international agreements for debt relief, a number of donor governments have undertaken to cancel debt unilaterally. The UK, for example, has cancelled all debts that arose from its international aid, both for the poorest countries and for some other Commonwealth countries, mostly in the Caribbean. And for HIPC countries that have not yet completed the process, the British government is saving up their debt repayments to return to them when they do complete it. The UK also supports nine non-HIPC countries by helping them pay debt service to the World Bank or the African Development Bank.

While the debt relief for the poorest countries is welcome, this does nothing for many other countries that are seriously in debt but do not meet the criteria because they are not poor enough or because their debt is considered sustainable in relation to export earnings. Nevertheless, for some of these countries debt represents a significant burden. In the Philippines, for example, between 1984 and 2007 total external debt rose from $24 billion to $62 billion and the government has been spending around $10 billion in debt service. Peru's debt stands at $28 billion which costs around $6 billion each year to service. In both cases this represents around one third of government budgets, and more than they spend on health and education combined.

This raises the question of what constitutes sustainability. The London-based New Economics Foundation (NEF) argues that developing countries should only service debt to the extent that this does not increase poverty or compromise future development. This means that they should not be putting the demands of creditors above the needs of their people. Assuming an 'ethical poverty line' of $3 per person, and based on data from 136 countries, the NEF concludes that up to 54 countries require complete cancellation of their debts, and between 32 and 53 countries need partial cancellation. This would involve total cancellation of between $424 billion and $589 billion – around one third of all developing country debt. This may seem a huge sum, but if the donor countries had kept their promises, made in 1970 at the UN General Assembly, to contribute 0.7 per cent of their GDPs as aid this would have generated an extra $120 billion a year, which would soon have wiped out the debt.[6]

The ugly sisters

Illegitimate and odious

In addition there is the broader question of whether these debts are even legitimate. Debts might be considered illegitimate for many reasons. The lenders may, for example, have been aware that the project was not viable or could have mis-sold or 'pushed' loans or demanded extortionate rates of interest. Often, they have lent funds to corrupt dictatorships which have squandered or pocketed them. In the Philippines, for example, between 1965 and 1986 Ferdinand Marcos added $27 billion to the country's debt, much of which he stole or wasted on useless projects like the notorious Bataan nuclear power plant which was built in an earthquake-prone zone next to a volcano. In most cases, the lenders were well aware of the character of the regimes they were supporting, so must take prime responsibility for this recklessness and the creation of

---

Odious debt

Odious debt is created by undemocratic governments that have seized power or are deeply corrupt – such as the Duvaliers in Haiti, Mobutu in former Zaire, or to those such as Suharto in Indonesia, who used some of the money usefully but redirected much of the rest into the pockets of his family or cronies. Odious debt is not a new concept, it was first raised in 1927 by Alexander Sack, a Russian jurist, who was the first to define this as debt contracted against the interests of the state's people, without their consent, and with full awareness of the creditor.

The idea resurfaced in recent years, particularly after 2003 when the US proposed cancelling Iraq's debt initially on the grounds that it had been accumulated by a dictator, Saddam Hussain. Iraq's debt was indeed subsequently cancelled but on the grounds of 'unsustainability'. Then in 2006, the Norwegian government cancelled $80 million in official debt owed to it by Ecuador, Egypt, Jamaica, Peru, and Sierra Leone, on the grounds that the real purpose of the loans had been to boost the Norwegian ship-building industry. The Norwegian government also funded an UNCTAD study on the legal basis of the concept which found that obligations to repay debt have 'frequently been limited or qualified by a range of equitable considerations, some of which may be regrouped under the concept of "odiousness"'.

Howse, R. 2007. *The concept of odious debt in international law*. UNCTAD Discussion Paper, No 185, Geneva, UNCTAD.

illegitimate 'odious debt' that subsequent regimes may reasonably repudiate (see box *Odious debt*).

What would happen if odious debt were acknowledged as illegitimate? The NEF has assessed some implications for a sample of ten countries that have had odious regimes – Argentina, the Democratic Republic of Congo, Ghana, Haiti, Malawi, Nicaragua, Nigeria, Pakistan, Peru, Philippines, South Africa and Sudan. Collectively, the odious debts they have accumulated since the 1960s amount to $726 billion. Since they have subsequently paid the debt down to around $345 billion, this means they have overpaid by $366 billion so should be asking for their money back. Indonesia, for example, has already overpaid by $150 billion and Argentina by $77 billion.[7]

While not quite asking for their money back, a number of governments and civil society groups in developing countries have at times launched inquiries into the legitimacy of their current debts. In 2008 for example, the government of Ecuador audited all of the country's debt contracts between 1976 and 2006. It found widespread malfeasance, and threatened to default on $3.9 billion worth of illegitimate bonds.[8] In the same year, Filipino organizations launched a People's Petition calling for the creation of an Independent Citizen's Debt Audit.

Not surprisingly, the World Bank, which is a serial odious lender, disputes all this. It argues that once countries start repudiating sovereign debts they will start to borrow recklessly in the knowledge that they can subsequently repudiate – a form of moral hazard.[9] It also points out that recognizing the concept would stop it making many loans in what it delicately terms 'challenging contexts'.[10] Quite so.

The situation is different for debts to banks and other commercial creditors. A few banks, in the spirit of the HIPC initiative, have joined in the process and extinguished the debt of HIPC countries, which could in total contribute to around 6 per cent of the relief, around $5 billion. Often this involves the World Bank buying the debt at a discount and then extinguishing it. In 2007, the World Bank approved a buyback that would eliminate most of Nicaragua's remaining $1.4 billion-worth of eligible commercial external debt.

Watch out for vultures

Other commercial creditors have proved less forgiving. A survey by the IMF in 2007 revealed that eleven countries facing a total of 44 creditors had been targeted with lawsuits.[11] The countries in the firing line included Nicaragua, the Republic of Congo (Congo Brazzaville), and Uganda. Most of the companies demanding repayment came from the United States, the United Kingdom, and the British Virgin Islands. Of these 24 won their cases – and though the original debts amounted to only $434 million, the judgments, which incorporated unpaid interest and other costs, amounted to around $1 billion.

Some of these litigants are 'vulture funds' or, as they prefer to be known, 'distressed-debt investors'. These are hedge funds or private equity funds which buy debt at knock-down price from banks who believe their borrowers are unlikely to pay up but do not have the stomach to chase them. Vulture funds swoop, then pursue the debtors mercilessly through the courts (see box *The vultures swoop*).

They have understandably come in for widespread condemnation. In 2002, Gordon Brown, then UK Chancellor of the Exchequer, said that the activity of the vulture funds led to 'morally outrageous' outcomes. Prior to their 2007 summit the G-8 finance ministers said: 'We are concerned about the actions of some litigating creditors against Heavily Indebted Poor Countries'. So far, however, there has been no specific action. One possibility would be legislation in the UK and the US to prevent litigation that counters

The vultures swoop

Vulture funds buy the debt of developing countries at a discount and then pursue the debtors ruthlessly through the courts for the full amount, or more. One of the largest is the $10 billion-hedge fund, Elliott Associates, run by billionaire Paul Singer. In 1996, for example, through one of its subsidiary companies, Kensington International, Elliott went after the Republic of Congo, purchasing from banks $30 million-worth of loans very cheaply, probably for less than 7 cents on the dollar.* Congo had defaulted and the banks were happy to sell even at this price for what otherwise would be impressive looking but useless sheets of paper. Kensington, which is registered in the Cayman Islands, took Congo to court in the UK, the US and elsewhere and was awarded a judgement of $199 million.**

Although the vultures usually buy sovereign debt from commercial creditors they have also been known to sink their talons into bilateral debt. In the 1970s Romania sold police vehicles and tractors worth $15 million to Zambia on credit. The deal was never that successful: the police vehicles broke down after six months so the Zambians refused to pay. In 1999, Donegal International, a subsidiary of Debt Advisory International, bought the debt for $3.3 million. Although Donegal sued for $56 million it was eventually awarded $16 million – in an infamous case that brought the vultures to public attention (Oxfam supporters demonstrated outside the court with a live vulture).

As well as being immensely lucrative for the vultures, this is also good business for lawyers, especially in London. Donegal was represented by Allen & Overy and collected $4 million in fees. Allen & Overy also worked for another vulture fund, Walker International, registered in the British Virgin Islands, which bought $21 million in Congo debt and was eventually awarded $48 million. Allen & Overy is proud of its corporate responsibility and pro bono work. It is a partner in Advocates for International Development (A4ID) which says it 'facilitates free legal assistance to civil society, developing country governments, social enterprises and bar associations to help achieve the UN MDGs'. Other A4ID partners include Decherts, which represents Kensington International, and Weil Gotshal & Manges, which helped Elliott Associates in one of its first actions, against Peru.***

*Hammer, J. 2008. 'Vultures of profit', in *Condé Nast Portofolio*, July www.portfolio.com

** IDA/IMF, 2007. *Heavily Indebted Poor Countries (HIPC) Initiative and Multilateral Debt Relief Initiative (MDRI)—Status of Implementation*, Washington. International Development Association and International Monetary Fund,

***Seager, A and J Lewis. 2007. *How top London law firms help vulture funds devour their prey*, in *The Guardian*, 17 October.

government policy on support for debt and poverty reduction.[12]

The Asian financial crisis

Debt is not the only consequence of having large amounts of capital washing around the world. Another is massive financial instability. Classical economic theory suggests that if businesses have the choice of borrowing both locally and overseas then a larger and more diverse 'capital market' will create some kind of equilibrium allowing for stable and predictable flows.

The real world is a lot messier, and more abrupt. Investors may in some cases carefully choose among a wide range of options, but just as often they tend to stampede suddenly as a herd. And just as bankers prefer to lend money to people who already have it, so investors generally crowd together and share waves of enthusiasm for a promising destination whether or not it needs the money. They then pile in to buy shares in the local stock exchange, or apartment buildings or office blocks. In order to do this, they have to buy local currency and thus push up the exchange rate. Soon the real economy starts to suffer: the high exchange rate makes exports more expensive while the lucky rich are bingeing on cheap imports. Then as soon as people realize that the party is over and it is time to leave, foreigners flock to the exits – cashing in their assets and selling the local currency which then spirals back downwards.

This was to be played out in Asia in the late 1990s when foreign investors poured into countries such as Thailand, Malaysia and Indonesia, attracted by fast growth, more or less fixed exchange rates and few financial controls. Moreover, most of the authoritarian Asian governments would clamp down on labor disputes and depress wages while allowing investors to send home their profits. Not surprisingly, businesses and speculators rushed in. Unfortunately much of the money was used for dubious investments that typically drove up real estate prices. Inevitably reality bit. In 1997 the funds started to flee Thailand and the Thai baht crashed, triggering a toppling of dominoes across the region, as investors took fright there too – from Malaysia to Indonesia, to the Republic of Korea (South Korea). Then, as now, banks that had made reckless loans for bad real estate investment had to be bailed out. In Indonesia, the government had to issue bonds to the value of $70 billion to inject local banks with sufficient capital. A modest sum by the standards required in 2008 to rescue Western banks, but a huge and immediate burden on the Indonesian poor – since to pay the interest rates on the bonds the government had to divert funds away from social expenditure.

Within about one year, the IMF was called in to finance rescue packages across the world of around $200 billion. Even if speculative money did not cause all the problems, it did ensure global contagion. But still the IMF and the World Bank continued to preach the virtues of open capital markets and cutting public expenditure – pushing their debtors on a further downward spiral. Countries in Asia that largely escaped were those such as China and India which had maintained capital controls, and Malaysia, which had ignored the IMF and slapped on new controls, and as a result emerged from the crisis much more quickly than other countries in the region.[13]

Eventually the IMF was to recant, at least partially, and admit that while allowing capital to move freely was right in theory, this did not often work in the imperfect world. But by then the damage had been done, and not just to the poor of Indonesia or Thailand but to the IMF itself. Nowadays, if they get the chance, countries will pay off their debts to the IMF quickly, to end a disastrous relationship. In 2005, Brazil paid off its $15.5 billion debt, rapidly followed by Argentina ($9.0 billion) and Uruguay ($630 million).[14]

The ugly sisters

Sisters in trouble

Many countries now prefer to build up huge foreign exchange reserves partly to make sure that they do not need to talk to the IMF. As a result, the boot is on the other foot. As fewer people borrow, the IMF's own income is cut. Like the World Bank, it pays itself from the difference between what it pays member countries that deposit funds and what it charges the borrowers. By mid 2008, with fewer loans outstanding and high staff costs, it was losing around $400 million a year and planning to cut its staff by around 15 per cent – a taste of its own bitter medicine.[15] To keep the wolf from the door it had to sell some 400 tons of gold – about one eighth of its reserves.

For the IMF, the 2008 financial dramas came as something of a relief, since it was able to lend some funds to desperate governments. Even then it was not the first port of call. Iceland, for example, whose freewheeling banks managed to bankrupt the whole country, was seeking help anywhere it could, even from Russia, before biting the bullet and taking a loan from the IMF. Other countries are now also returning to the Fund, though it is noticeable that they no longer face such rigid conditions for loans.

The World Bank too has steadily been losing its rationale. Its original purpose now seems out of date. The middle-income countries like India can just as easily get long-term loans by selling their own bonds. And it seems strange that the World Bank is still lending to China, a total of $1.5 billion by 2008, when China already has $1.6 trillion in foreign exchange reserves which it has been using to buy US securities, dabble on the Hong Kong stock exchange, and hoover up US companies.[16] The reason of course is that, like any bank, the World Bank has to constantly push out more loans just to keep afloat. It claims that the small profit it makes on such pointless loans gets passed on to poor countries. But even many poorer countries are now by-passing the

World Bank. Sudan and the Democratic Republic of the Congo, for example, find it easier to get funds from China and India which are distributing largesse around Africa, with no strings attached, in order to secure future supplies of oil and minerals.

The outlook for the World Bank thus seems uncertain. One likely scenario is that it could close its IBRD operations and confine itself to making concessional IDA loans. This would, however, make it much less independent, and wealthy, since it would have to turn regularly to donor governments to replenish its funds. In any case both institutions were fairly impotent in the face of the 2008 financial collapse, which is the subject of the next chapter.

1 Woods, N. 2006. *The Globalizers: the IMF, the World Bank, and their borrowers*. Ithaca and London. Cornell University Press. 2 Peet, R. 2003. *Unholy Trinity: the IMF, World Bank and WTO*. London and New York, Zed Books. 3 JDC, 2008. *Unfinished business: Ten years of dropping the debt*. London, Jubilee Debt Campaign. www.jubileedebtcampaign.org.uk 4 Loser, C. 2004. *External Debt Sustainability: Guidelines for Low- and Middle-income Countries*, G-24 Discussion Paper Series No. 24. Geneva, UNCTAD. 5 HM Treasury, 2008. www.hm-treasury.gov.uk/documents/international_issues/international_development/development_facts.cfm 6 NEF 2006. *Debt relief as if people mattered*, London, New Economics Foundation. 7 NEF, 2006, *Debt relief as if justice mattered*, London, New Economics Foundation. 8 *The Economist*, 2008. 'Can pay, might not', in *The Economist*, 27 November. 9 Nehru, V and Thomas, M. 2008. *The concept of odious debt: some considerations*, Policy Research working paper; WPS 4676, Washington, World Bank. 10 World Bank, 2008. Meeting Note. *Round Table on Conceptual and Operational Issues of Lender Responsibility for Sovereign Debt*, Washington DC, World Bank. 14 April 2008. 11 IDA/IMF, 2007. *Heavily Indebted Poor Countries (HIPC) Initiative and Multilateral Debt Relief Initiative (MDRI)—Status of Implementation*, Washington. International Development Association and International Monetary Fund. 12 Jones, M. 2007. '"Vulture funds" threat to developing world'. BBC website: news.bbc.co.uk 13 Stiglitz, J et al. 2006. *Stability with growth: Macroeconomics, liberalization and development*, New York, Oxford University Press, p 168. 14 Sarabia, M. 2007. Funding the IMF, University of Iowa, Center for International Development, Briefing paper. www.uiowa.edu/ifdebook/briefings/docs/imf.shtml. Accessed 10/10/08. 15 *The Economist*, 2008. 'It's Mostly Firing', *The Economist* 7 February. 16 Xinhua, 2008. 'World Bank's loans to China total $1.5 bln in 2008 fiscal year', *Xinhua News Agency*, 25 June.

7 Meltdown

The implosion that started in 2008 was a dramatic affair. Collapsing banks, panicking governments, and anxious savers wondering whether their funds were about to go up in smoke. As financial crises go, this was spectacular. And it certainly came as a shock. But it can hardly be considered a surprise.

INTERNATIONAL CAPITALISM, AND particularly finance, is inherently unstable. If you believed classical economic theory you might dispute this. In theory, efficient markets, left to their own devices, will reach a state of equilibrium where demand is forever balanced by supply – whether of goods, or services or money. In the case of money, however, this is never true. A system based on credit, which literally means 'belief', will like any human institution be prone to sudden shifts, from waves of optimism to sudden crises of confidence.[1]

These crises have become increasingly frequent. One study found that in the period 1949 to 1971 there were 48 financial crises around the world, but that in the period 1973 to 1997 there were 139.[2] They have also become increasingly serious: the way that financial markets have developed in recent years has amplified the normal mood swings of an economic cycle into full-blown manic depression. The latest global collapse has many origins. It has links, for example, with the Asian financial crisis of the late 1990s which taught many Asian countries that at all costs they should steer clear of the IMF; in future they should build up their own insurance by saving huge sums that could be parked in the United States. This may have seemed prudent, but has indirectly offered US citizens ready sources of easy money which they may or may not use wisely. The crisis also has links with efforts in the 1980s to regulate banks, requiring them to hold sufficient capital, which has had the perverse effect of encouraging them to devise ever more dangerous loopholes. It also has technological origins, notably in the availability of cheap computer power which has allowed financial wizards to conjure up astonishing piles of interlinked derivatives balanced precariously on the same shaky underlying assets.

The previous big bubble

A convenient starting point for the story is the year 2000. The stock markets were just recovering from a technological crash – the dotcom boom – another bubble that started in 1995 and was based on the blind faith that any company doing anything on this new internet thingy would be bound to make vast sums of money. Surely, it was thought, the normal rules no longer applied and any dotcom enterprise from pets. com to smells.com would grab enough global market share that its value would escalate forever into the stratosphere.

Stock values certainly rose quickly. The US stock exchange on which most dotcom stocks were traded, the NASDAQ, increased fivefold from 1995, when the internet browser Netscape was launched, to reach a giddy peak in March 2000. Then the bubble burst. Eighteen months later the NASDAQ was back where it started – wiping out $4.4 trillion dollars, at that time the largest stock market collapse in the history of industrial capitalism.[3]

The essential characteristic of this bubble like many others is the assumption that the value of something, from stock prices to houses, will rise forever. Even if you know this is nonsense, you can still make money on the way up, providing you get off the escalator before it tips you over a cliff. The problem, and thus the opportunity, is that no-one knows exactly when to step off.

Moreover the dotcom bubble was also to sow the seeds of the sub-prime disaster. Following the stock market crash the US Federal Reserve, anxious to get the economy moving again, rapidly pushed down interest rates, from 6.5 to 3.5 per cent. Then no sooner had Wall Street absorbed that drama than al-Qaeda appeared on the scene on September 11 2001. In response, the Fed lowered interest rates still further. By 2003, they were down to 1 per cent.

Here we go again

For several years US interest rates were below the rate of inflation – so real interest rates were negative. In these circumstances the sensible thing to do was to borrow as much as you could to buy something that would rise in value while the low cost of your loan was eroded by inflation. And what safer option could there be than buying your own home?

For most people buying a house is their largest-ever personal transaction. It is also the one most likely to be achieved with borrowed funds. Even the most prudent households do not blink at taking on a huge loan to buy a house, since the mortgage repayments appear similar to paying rent, with the crucial advantage that after 20 or 30 years you will finish up owning your home. House purchase is thus in financial terms a highly 'leveraged' but apparently safe transaction.

Like any other leveraged activity, however, the viability of house purchasing is acutely sensitive to changes in interest rates. As interest rates stayed low, not just in the US but in many other countries, people became much more attracted by the prospect of buying their own house or even a second or third one to rent out. In response, house prices in many countries, particularly the US, the UK, Spain and France, started to shoot up (see graphic *(Un)safe as houses*).

The effect of housing bubbles will depend to some extent on the nature of the mortgages. In the UK the bank or building society will probably take the deeds of the property as security. Nevertheless, the borrower

(Un)safe as houses

Between 2000 and 2005, in the developed countries the total value of residential property rose from $40 trillion to $70 trillion.* This is illustrated here for the United Kingdom which shows average house prices, adjusted for inflation, over the period 1976 to 2008.** A house that in 1976 was worth £62,000, in today's pounds, was worth £193,000 by 2007.

Inflation-adjusted house prices in the UK, 1976-2008

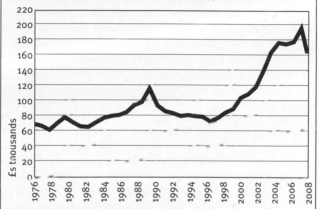

* *The Economist*, 2005. 'In come the waves', in *The Economist*, 16 June.

**Nationwide, 2008. Nationwide house price index, at www.nationwide.co.uk/hpi/default.asp

Source: Nationwide, 2008

still remains liable for the full amount of the loan. This is called a 'recourse loan'. In the 1980s the housing boom in the UK was followed by a sudden collapse which left many people paying mortgages for properties that had lost value – they were in 'negative equity'. If the monthly interest charges became unpayable, they could not simply sell the house since the proceeds would no longer cover the loan. This was enough to force many households into bankruptcy.

Another serious implication of a house price boom is that it dramatically increases inequality. If you are lucky enough to own a house at the beginning of the boom then you will make a huge unearned profit if you choose to sell. But if you are a young first-time buyer, then things are much more difficult since even if interest rates are low, you will find it difficult to borrow enough to get on the housing ladder.

Irresponsible lenders

When housing prices are rising faster than incomes, responsible lenders then struggle to find customers to lend to. This should in theory act as a restraint. If there are no new buyers then prices should stabilize. But what about irresponsible lenders? Unfortunately the US managed to devise a system through which, despite soaring house prices, many of the poorest people were still able to buy.

This involved using a series of intermediaries who effectively cut the lines of communication between the borrowers and the ultimate lenders. Previously, when a bank manager lent funds to buy a house he or she needed to make sure the borrower repaid. But in recent years, the people in the US who were providing the funds had very little idea of who they were lending to, and how risky the loans were.

The first links in the chain were the mortgage brokers who, working on commission, signed up new borrowers. By 2003, they were running out of potential new house owners, since no-one could afford to buy on the usual terms. The brokers thus had to devise ever more seductive arrangements to sign up people who were poor credit risks – the 'sub-prime' borrowers. They devised schemes which included, for example, charging very low interest rates at the outset, with little or no down payment, but having a high rate kick in later. And rather than asking for evidence of income, they would take borrowers at their word – 'self-certification'. The results were often 'ninja' loans – to people with no income, no job, no assets.

Borrowers went along with this, either because they had no idea of what they were committing themselves to, or because they reasoned that with house prices rising continuously they would later be able to sell at a profit. This seemed like a one-way bet. A further encouragement was that in some cases mortgages in the US, particularly in California, are 'non-recourse' loans, which means that ultimately you can just send the bank the keys to the house, 'jingle mail', leaving the bank with no further claim on you. The outcome of all this was that a steadily increasing proportion of loans was going to sub-prime borrowers who were likely to default. Between 2001 and 2005 the total value of sub-prime loans rose from around 5 per cent of the total to around 20 per cent.[4]

Insecure securitization

You can see why the borrowers and the brokers might collude in this ever slacker lending system. But what of the banks? They after all are regulated and there are limits to the loans they can make. According to the Basel agreements, for every loan they add to their balance sheets, they need to have sufficient capital to serve as a buffer against borrowers defaulting. Unfortunately, while the Basel rules promised to make banks seem safer, they had the perverse effect of encouraging their financial wizards to find ways around the rules – to push the loans off their balance sheets.

Here the key was 'securitization' – converting mortgage repayments into securities that acted like bonds. As an illustrative aside, it is worth noting that anything that produces a fairly predictable flow of income can be sold as a security. One of the most notable was in 1997 when David Bowie sold $55 million-worth of 'Bowie Bonds' which entitled the buyers to a share in the revenue from his first 25 albums over a period of ten years.[5] Unfortunately Bowie's earnings did not prove as high as expected and by 2004 Moody's Investor Service was rating these at a little above junk status.

Mortgages too should produce a steady stream of

income. But since converting only one or two mortgages into a security would produce a security too dependent on the reliability of individual borrowers, a bank can then spread the risk by packaging a large number of mortgages together. Through a series of maneuvers it creates a new security with the clumsy name of a 'collateralized debt obligation' (CDO) and sells this to a specially created company, a 'special purpose vehicle' (SPV), which will then sell the CDO to investors (see box *Collateralized debt obligations*). The bank still collects the mortgage payments, for a suitable fee, and passes them on to the SVP which in turn passes them to the owners of the CDOs. But the loans are no longer on the bank's balance sheet. As the jargon has it, the bank has moved from an 'originate-to-hold' to an 'originate-to distribute' model. With those loans off its

---

Collateralized debt obligations

Banks can offload their dodgy mortgages by pooling them as securities which they can then pass on to investors. This involves first creating a new intermediate company or trust – a 'special purpose vehicle' (SPV) – which is legally independent from the bank. For example, a bank may have $200 million in a collection of mortgages that might be delivering 6 per cent – $12 million per year. It then sells this package to the SPV which borrows funds in the money markets for this purpose until it can sell the $200 million package to investors. The package is sold in tranches. If there were three tranches, say, then the senior tranche, which might involve 70 per cent of the issue, would have first call on all the income, and have the highest AAA rating, but offer the lowest yield. A second tranche would be next in line for a payout if there is enough cash coming in, but offer a higher yield. The bottom tranche, the 'toxic waste', and the equivalent of junk bonds, would offer the highest yield but be the first to be excluded from payments if there are defaults.

Nevertheless, everyone remains exposed to the complete package. The AAA tranche does not correspond to good mortgages, but only to first priority of payment on the basis of the package as a whole. It does not take many mortgage owners sending 'jingle mail' (returning the house keys to the bank) for these apparently safe AAA securities to tumble down the ratings alphabet – and trigger a general financial panic.

balance sheet, either the bank does not need to maintain so much capital, or it can use the proceeds from the sale to make more profitable loans.

A crucial feature of the CDOs is the way they are structured. The whole package is presented to buyers in difference slices, or 'tranches'. The top tranches offer the greater security but lower income, while the lowest tranches, the 'toxic waste', offer the highest returns if the whole package performs well but also risk providing no income at all if too many mortgage holders default. Note that the top tranches do not correspond to the best mortgages since the package is considered as a whole, so owners of all the tranches are exposed one way or another to all the mortgages.

For the investors, the advantage is that they can become players in the domestic mortgage market without the messy business of selling loans or collecting arrears. They can also rely on the ratings agencies to provide information about the various tranches to enable them to decide just how much risk to take on – the 'safe' AAA tranches at the top, perhaps, or the CCC tranches at the bottom, which are the equivalent of high-yielding junk bonds. The rating agencies too make money on this. By 2003, structured finance was accounting for 40 to 50 per cent of the income of agencies such as Moody's or Fitch.[6] Mind you, the ratings agencies relied for information on the issuers of CDOs, since they were in no position to fully assess these highly complex products themselves.

The effect of all this has been to further distance the borrower from the lender. Everybody along the chain follows their own interest. The borrowers get a loan to buy a house. The mortgage brokers pick up their commissions on each sale. The banks take fees for setting up and servicing the loan contracts. The investors get a range of juicy looking securities.

Structured mortgage finance took off in a big way. And the structures soon became ever more complex.

Meltdown

Originally a single issue might have three or four differently rated tranches, but soon the numbers soared into the hundreds. Then all sorts of complications and elaborations entered the mix. Not just combinations of fixed- and floating-rate mortgages, but other types of derivatives such as credit default swaps. Then the wizards started to create even more devious spells by mixing tranches from different packages – CDO^2s. They even conjured up weird CDO^3s.

The securities houses were also churning out more conventional CDOs based on other assets that could deliver a regular income, such as credit card loans, or commercial property. But by 2006 most of the CDOs were being issued for domestic property loans of which around two-thirds were sub-prime. In the 1980s the securities dealers would have had to run their mainframes for days to compute who was entitled to what payment. But over the next 20 years the rapid development of personal computers and workstations would soon make light work of the calculations.

The bubble bursts

But what did this all mean? Ultimately only the people who devised the models for constructing the CDOs knew what went into them, and even they would be unable to predict the outcome of all scenarios. Sitting in the boardrooms, the directors of banks, insurance companies and pension schemes saw only the glossy prospectuses listing securities that would offer higher yields than other comparably rated corporate bonds. The problem of course was that all these superimposed computerized constructions were resting on dubious foundations. The various tranches only achieved their high ratings because historically during a time of rising house prices the number of mortgage defaults, even on sub-prime loans, was low. The result was that a clever CDO-maker could devise an issue with 80 per cent of its bonds rated AAA or AA when in fact more than 70 per cent of the underlying assets were sub-prime.[7]

You might wonder what the US government was doing during this period. After all, a central bank is supposed to worry about inflation and raise interest rates accordingly. But inflation in the US remained persistently low. This was partly because the supply of cheap goods from Asia was keeping prices down, and Asian countries which were recycling their funds into US government bonds were keeping the dollar high which further depressed the cost of imports for US consumers.

But what about house prices? They did not enter the picture. Conventionally, inflation figures only incorporate the prices of goods and services; they do not include the prices of 'assets' such as houses. Indeed, central banks have usually regarded asset price bubbles as outside their area of responsibility. Some would even argue that there is no such thing as a bubble: if the market dictates a certain price for a house then that is the end of the story. In fact the then chair of the Federal Reserve, Alan Greenspan, encouraged people to take out home loans. The conventional view was that it was impossible to distinguish a bubble from an underlying rise in asset prices.

Meanwhile, in the real world

Out in the real world, the mortgage brokers could have told Greenspan something different. They were running out of people to whom they could legitimately sell new loans so were making increasingly perilous offers. These were still packaged into safe-looking bonds because in a rising market defaults even for sub-prime loans had been quite small. But once the brokers finally pushed buyers over the edge the defaults started to rise. Because of the structure of the bonds even a small increase in defaults could trigger a reduced rating for all the tranches – even the supposedly secure ones at the top. But still the Fed paid little attention.

Meltdown

The bubble had to burst, and in 2007 it duly did. The first sequence of pops emerged from the hedge funds. As is their usual style they had borrowed huge sums to load up with those high-yielding sub-prime CDOs. When the ratings of these suddenly started to slip they were in trouble, and since they held huge quantities even small drops in value were leveraged or magnified into huge potential losses. Overnight in some cases many AAA rated bonds were downgraded to junk.

Another characteristic of many of these derivative markets is that they are private 'over-the-counter' deals. The CDOs are not traded on exchanges. This means that there is no public record of who owns what, and no-one is ever sure of the market price. Moreover with no exchange, there may be no ready buyer. Among the first to panic was the investment bank Bear Stearns which owned a couple of hedge funds and found itself saddled with near worthless CDOs. Suddenly it started selling anything it could. As there was no market for the CDOs, it had to dispose of everything else. Thus a crisis that started in the housing market was suddenly transmitted to other areas of a complex, interlinked financial system.

This crisis also then started to hit the banks. They had securitized the mortgages off their balance sheets only to see many of them make an unwelcome return. In some cases this was because they had issued the CDOs with a guarantee against any heavy defaults occurring soon after issue – so as the defaults rose the buyers claimed their money back and the toxic sludge oozed back onto the banks' balance sheets. Other mortgages returned to the banks through the back door in the form of loans to risky hedge funds which had bought CDOs. The extent of entanglement between financial institutions is difficult to appreciate. Banks may, for example, hold corporate bonds but have taken the precaution of insuring these via credit default swaps, only to find that the suppliers of these swaps, the 'counterparties', are institutions to which they have made loans.[8] Oh dear.

Rock and a hard place

This is where we reach the credit crunch. The banks are running scared. Since no-one really knows who owes what to whom, suddenly nobody wants to lend to anybody for fear that their counterparty will go bust. The usual process of lending between banks grinds to a halt. The 'money markets', consisting of banks and other big institutions lending short-term funds, are desperate to hang on to what they have got – and if they do lend at all they will charge cripplingly high interest rates. That's OK if you have plenty of cash; you can largely sit tight. If not, even if you are solvent you may be in trouble.

Enter the British bank Northern Rock. Ironically Northern Rock was to be brought to its knees not by risky lending to the British equivalent of sub-prime borrowers but by its own risky borrowing. The former building society concentrated on lending money to commercial landlords, or individuals who were buying property to let. Since it could not gather enough funds from its depositors for this purpose it had to look elsewhere.

Like the US banks, Northern Rock turned to securitization, through an offshore special purpose vehicle called, somewhat optimistically, Granite. But it also borrowed short-term funds on the money markets, partly to finance the operations of Granite until it sold the bonds, but also just for general use to finance mortgages. The strategy was to get 25 per cent of funds from savers, 50 per cent from securitization, and 25 per cent from the money markets.[9] What the clever managers of Northern Rock never bargained for was that the money markets would seize up – and refuse to renew their loans on any terms.

Meltdown

Northern Rock thus had thousands of mortgages but no way of funding them. In September 2008 it had to ask the Bank of England for help. Savers heard the news and took fright, though being British they formed orderly queues for their 'run on the bank'. The British government dithered, then made loans to tide the bank over, but six months later had to nationalize it to keep it afloat.

Elsewhere too the dominoes were starting to topple. In October 2007the giant Swiss bank UBS said it had lost $3.4 billion in sub-prime investments (later revised to $37 billion). In March 2008 Bear Stearns, which a year earlier had been valued at around $40 billion, was bought by JPMorgan Chase for just $240 million. In the UK, the Royal Bank of Scotland soon found itself running short of capital.

Meltdown

By mid-2008, the threat of total financial meltdown had spurred governments into dramatic action. At first they thought they could prop up the banks by extending credit to tide them over the crises and the US Federal Reserve came up with a $700-billion package. But it soon became clear that this would not suffice. Many banks were becoming not just illiquid but insolvent. They needed more capital, and so would have to issue more shares which only governments were in a position to buy – resulting in total or complete nationalization. In September 2008 the US government announced it was taking over the country's two giant housing corporations, the Federal National Mortgage Association, nicknamed Fannie Mae, and the Federal Home Mortgage Corporation, Freddie Mac.

In the UK the government then nationalized the Bradford and Bingley bank and in October announced it was taking stakes in many other banks including Lloyds TSB, the Royal Bank of Scotland and HBOS – to the tune of around £37 billion. Taxpayers would own 60 per cent of the Royal Bank of Scotland and 40 per cent of the merged Lloyds TSB and HBOS.

Meanwhile in the US, the government had declined to rescue the country's fourth largest investment bank, Lehman Brothers, which duly went bust, with huge repercussions for its counterparty banks, while the largest investment bank, Merrill Lynch, was taken over by Bank of America. Eventually, with other banks in peril, the Treasury Secretary followed the British lead and in October announced that the government would spend $250 billion on part-nationalizing a number of American banks and the main insurance company AIG. Socialism had come to America.

The rest of the world takes a hit

Although most of the drama was taking place in the US and the UK, which had the world's leading financial centers, the rest of the world felt the pain. In the first instance this was because banks and other institutions which needed to raise cash, and could not sell their 'toxic' assets, instead had to sell the healthy ones which included shares in companies in developing countries, or 'emerging markets' which had attracted large flows of investment.

Moreover, the sub prime mortgages themselves continued to cause damage in the most unlikely places. In Singapore and Hong Kong it turned out in late 2008 that more than 50,000 small investors, desperate to get slightly better returns for their pension nest eggs, had been sold 'Lehman mini-bonds' – incredibly complex structures that included a good dose of subprime backed CDOs. In November 2008, thousands of them took to the streets to protest at the loss of their savings.[10]

But for most of the world's poor the damage is being caused by a crashing global economy. Lower prices for commodities are already affecting many African countries, and across Asia growth is slackening, throwing thousands of people out of work. A crisis triggered by irresponsible lending in the United States is having global repercussions. Are there not better ways of organizing the global financial system? That is the subject of the final chapter.

1 Cooper, G. 2008. *The Origin of Financial Crises: Central Banks, credit bubbles and the efficient market fallacy*. Petersfield, Harriman House. 2 Bordo, M and B. Eichengreen, 2002. *Crisis Now and Then: What Lessons from the Last Era of Financial Globalization*, Cambridge Mass., National Bureau of Economic Research, Working Paper 8716. 3 Goldfarb, B, D Kirsch and D Miller, 2006. *Was there too little entry during the Dot Com Era?*, Robert H Smith School of Business, University of Maryland. Working Paper No. RHS-06-029. http://ssrn.com/abstract=899100 4 Morris, C. 2008. *The Trillion Dollar Meltdown*, New York, Public Affairs. 5 WSJ, 2005 'Bankers Hope for a Reprise Of "Bowie Bonds"', in *The Wall Street Journal*, 23 August. 6 BIS, 2005. *The role of ratings in structured finance: issues and implications*. Committee on the Global Financial System. Basel, Bank for International Settlements 7 Morris, C. 2008. *The Trillion Dollar Meltdown*, New York, Public Affairs, p 78. 8 *The Economist*, 2007.' Prime movers', in *The Economist*, 9 April. 9 Walters, B. 2008. *The fall of Northern Rock*, Petersfield, Harriman House. 10 *The Economist*, 2008. 'Thanks, Hank', in *The Economist*, 20 November.

8 Starting afresh

Money is too important to be left to bankers, whose greed and incompetence have resulted in a financial system capable of delivering them grotesque incomes but exposing everyone else to massive risk. Time to start again, treating banking as a public utility that should be as tightly regulated as any other.

BANKS EXIST FOR the simple purpose of connecting savers and borrowers, of making the best use of scarce resources. Even in the traditional model there was an inherent risk in promising savers that they could withdraw their funds whenever they liked while simultaneously promising borrowers that they could keep the same funds for 20 years or more to build a business or buy a house. There was always the possibility that both groups would exercise their rights simultaneously, alarming investors and triggering a run on the bank. By and large this risk proved manageable. With sufficient guarantees of savings in place, and the capacity of the central bank to act as a lender of last resort this scenario arose only rarely. In the UK the crisis in Northern Rock was the first major bank run in 90 years.

Over the last 20 years, however, a relatively straightforward financial model has become hugely more complex, as banks and other financial institutions have devised ever more intricate interlocking forms of investment and borrowing. They would argue that they have done so in order to respond to market demand, creating opportunities for investors and borrowers that offer different combinations of cost and risk to meet every need – from those of the pensioners trying to conserve their nest eggs to those the high-rolling hedge fund gamblers willing to stake millions of dollars in single transaction. The consequences included steep rises in stock and property prices – very welcome to those who owned stocks or houses, even if they did not appreciate how this boom could lead to a massive bust.

Governments, who should have known better, have largely stood aside, and have chosen to deregulate the financial sector – giving the bankers free rein to dream up multiple new schemes, however impenetrable. The financial sector was also a rich source of income. In the UK the government welcomed a steady flow of funds via taxation: by 2004 the financial sector, although constituting only one tenth of national output, was contributing more than one quarter of corporation tax revenues. Then there was the income tax from all those high-earning traders. Between 1997 and 2006, the number of people earning over £100,000, many of whom worked in the City of London, had risen to 500,000, increasing their tax contribution over the same period from £10 billion to £34 billion –from 13 per cent to one quarter of all income tax revenue.[1]

This gives the mistaken impression that the financiers are creating new wealth. In reality they are just taking other people's money. If you save or borrow through a building society or a credit union or any other form of mutual system, you will get a lower savings rate than is charged to borrowers – there is always a 'spread'. This is understandable since the organization that brings savers and borrowers together has to pay administration and wage costs. The financial services industry for all its presumed sophistication ultimately does much the same thing, except that it multiplies the number of intermediaries and their salaries – and therefore the spread. From hedge funds to investment banks they are doing the same thing as a credit union, borrowing and lending, but by devising many new ways of gathering and dispersing money they have been able to grab more of the spread for themselves.

The value that underpins financial earnings depends

finally on workers and entrepreneurs operating businesses to provide goods and services. Over the longer term this has created 'real' returns in the stock market of around five per cent per year. In recent years, however, the financial services industry has been taking a larger cut of this. This has been termed the 'croupier's take' – the amount skimmed off by investment banks, by various brokers, traders, operators of mutual funds, and financial advisers, who between them grab between 40 and 80 per cent of the money that might otherwise have gone to investors.[2]

This dense thicket of transactions is usually justified on the grounds that it meets with exquisite precision the needs of borrowers and investors, as perfect financial markets respond to subtle shifts in supply and demand. But the financial markets are far from perfect. No-one knows fully what is going on, even in publicly traded shares. However, some participants have insider information: corporate managers and the traders have a far better idea than investors – an imbalance referred to as 'asymmetry of information' – and use this to their own advantage.

Awe and shock
Another justification for all this financial innovation is that everyone is free to assume the degree of risk with which they are comfortable. Again this is a myth. Few people are capable of accurately assessing risk. Even the directors of investment funds have only the vaguest idea what their own staff are up to, and don't much care, as long as this month's profit figures are good. Governments too have been somewhat in awe of the financial wizards and have been proud of applying a light regulatory touch, arguing that the most dangerous arenas of speculation affect only sophisticated investors who know what they are doing and need little protection. As has become abundantly clear, however, while the high-rollers are willing to monopolize the

rewards of success, they have been more generous with the fruits of failure – forcing governments into rescue acts to stave off systemic collapses.

Much is made of the complexity and ingenuity of modern financial models. Perhaps judged by their own criteria they are sophisticated. But in fact complexity is often a sign of incompetence. Any computer programmer knows that it takes only two or three inept lines of code to generate unpredictable outcomes – and cause a computer to freeze. Similarly, some relatively straightforward operations on a ball of wool by the average cat will rapidly produce an almighty tangle of which the cat can be very proud. The global financial system is in a comparable mess, and is unsafe in the hands of bankers. What are the alternatives? There can be no single answer but there are at least some measures that would steer finance in a more productive direction.

Revoke licenses to print money

One of the more remarkable features of the financial system is that most of the money is made by banks. This is not just because they can make huge profits, but because they do create most of the money. Assuming that banks keep only 10 per cent of each deposit and lend the rest, then for each $100 deposited they add a further $900 to the stock of money (see box in Chapter 2, *How credit creates money*). A fundamental reorganization of global monetary systems should start at this point. A number of theorists have pointed out that allowing banks to create money is fundamentally unjust since it involves a massive and continuing transfer of resources from the public to the private sector.

As was explained in Chapter 2, monarchs and other rulers originally had the monopoly on issuing new money in the form of coins. Then private and later central banks stepped in, by issuing new coins and paper money. Governments could spend this into circulation, for example, by using it to pay soldiers or government officials. This privilege, of being able to make money and spend it, is known as 'seignorage'. Nowadays, however, coins and banknotes account for only around five per cent of the new money that appears. The rest materializes, as if by magic, when commercial banks make loans to their customers. The amount they can lend is limited only by how much of their own capital they retain to offset bad debts. In the past they have usually been happy to lend around ten times their capital, though in current circumstances this ratio has been reduced to seven or eight.[3]

The other creator of money is the central bank. In the UK for example, according to monetary theorist James Robertson, the government issues around £6 billion per year in coins and banknotes which it uses to pay its own bills. But this is dwarfed by the money created and extinguished by banks, which earns them around £40 billion per year in profits. If on the other hand new money for the British financial system could be created only by the Bank of England and spent into circulation by the government this would provide it with £90 billion a year to spend.[4] In other countries a similar system would be equivalent to $114 billion in the US, €160 billion in the euro area, and more than ¥17 trillion in Japan. These amounts are equivalent to between 5 and 15 per cent of tax revenues, enabling governments to boost public expenditure, cut taxes or distribute money to every citizen in the form of income entitlements.

Practicalities

How would this work? It would primarily require making a sharp distinction between the money in your current account for transactions and the money in savings accounts. In this new system when you put money into your current account (a 'sight deposit') this would act as a sort of holding box and thus pay no interest. As now, you could use the money to pay bills, either in cash or electronically. But this money would not appear on the balance sheet of the banks; it would be money that belongs to you, just like banknotes in your wallet.

Banks would continue to offer loans, but they would do so in a much simpler fashion. Anything they lend would have to come from money deposited with them by savers, or borrowed from other banks, or from their tills, or from their own accounts held at the central bank. In total this would not greatly change the functioning of banks but it would oblige them to operate in a more transparent fashion and under greater government control. They would continue to offer services, for a suitable fee, and make loans but would not be able to cream off extra profits by creating money.

This reform would also result in greater economic stability. For example, during an economic downturn bank customers tend to stop taking new loans, or will pay off old ones. In the existing system, just as creating new loans increases the stock of money, so paying off old ones diminishes it. Less money in circulation then tends to make the recession even worse, sending the economy on a downward spiral of deflation. In short, by lending money commercial banks tend to amplify both the peaks and troughs. But if the supply of money is effectively fixed by the central bank then as people repaid loans they would simply return it to its original owners so the stock of money would be unchanged.

Return to savings
In addition there should be other changes in the ways in which banks operate. In the relentless pursuit of profits banks have grown dissatisfied with the model of simply gathering funds from savers and instead have

turned to the wholesale money markets either to borrow the funds for mortgages and other loans or to securitize mortgages. The British bank Northern Rock pursued this strategy relentlessly and recklessly on the assumption that it could roll over its loans from the money markets whenever it wished. When the big lenders started to say no, everything fell to pieces.

Instead, banks should be required to make a much higher proportion of loans from deposits, and rather than securitizing them they should keep them on their own balance sheets so that both their customers and depositors are fully aware of the bank's situation. This would mean shifting from the originate-to-distribute model back to the originate-to-hold model. Banks also need to ensure that they retain sufficient capital – to be accumulated during boom years, rather than being paid out as huge bonuses or dividends, and held in reserve for economic downturns.

The financial meltdown has also raised questions about the ownership of banks. The whole or part nationalization of banks may have appeared surprising in free market economies in Europe and the United States. But this simply revealed an underlying truth that by operating with implicit or explicit state guarantees, banks are necessarily under the protective umbrella of national treasuries. The logical solution would be for banks to stay nationalized, or at least for some banks to remain in state hands to offer depositors and borrowers a different option. This would make it more difficult for the other banks to compete, as the subsequent success of the nationalized Northern Rock has demonstrated. So much the better.

Size matters

Another issue is the size of commercial banks. One of the legacies of the meltdown of 2008 is that it has resulted in a series of bank takeovers, as the ones still standing seized the opportunity to absorb those at death's door. The British government swatted away concerns about competition when it encouraged Lloyds TSB to take over HBOS. Part of the problem with banks is that most have grown too big to be allowed to fail. Instead they should be broken up so that none is large enough for its failure to pose a systemic risk. While the deposits of customers should be guaranteed, the survival of the bank should not be.

Even more alarming is that investment banks have become increasingly merged with retail banks into 'universal banks'. In the US this has involved some retail banks taking over investment banks and some investment banks applying for retail banking licenses. This is precisely the wrong direction. The two functions should be kept entirely separate since this puts retail depositors at risk when the investment arm gets into trouble or, more likely, cries for help to the weary taxpayer.

In all of this, bank customers should have the choice of which institutions to use – either a state-owned bank offering the greatest security, or a reasonably sized and well run commercial bank, or a credit union, or more likely a mixture of one or more.

Prune the exotica

The meltdown of 2008 and the ensuing economic recession it triggered can be laid firmly at the door of speculators in banks, hedge funds and other institutions who had created a shadow financial system, operating with intertwining and overlapping derivatives. Not only were these barely comprehended, even by those using them, the ways in which they would interact were almost impossible to predict. Some derivatives are useful; others are largely vehicles for speculation. All should be presented for inspection by the financial authorities and only those approved should be used – and traded on public exchanges so that everyone is aware of who owns what and which institution is exposed to what risk. Trading in unapproved derivatives would be stifled if these were legally unenforceable.

Among the most dangerous derivatives are credit default swaps, currently valued at around $55 trillion – an indirect and opaque form of insurance that could yet sink many more lenders.[5] These should be banned, requiring lenders to take full responsibility for the credit they offer and denying speculators this particular form of get-rich scheme.

Also in line for pruning should be the hedge funds. At present these are largely unregulated since it was wrongly assumed they were a risk only to themselves. One way to reduce the damage would be to prevent short selling by banning other institutions from lending them the shares they need for this purpose.

Tax the transactions

Distortions and bubbles of all kinds are encouraged by electronic trading which can see shares or currencies or bonds changing hands continuously at lightning speed. This encourages 'momentum' trading which has nothing to do with underlying values and more to do with what other traders will do in the subsequent seconds or minutes. One of the most promising ways of addressing this, but as yet untried 30 years after it was proposed by Nobel laureate James Tobin, would be to tax every transaction. At present only around 5 per cent of currency trades, around $3 trillion per day, are linked to actual trade. The rest is speculation which can wreak havoc with national budgets especially for developing countries.

Applying a sales tax of around 0.2 per cent on each trade would skim off much of the speculative froth – while also generating valuable revenue. Assuming the annual trade were cut to a more reasonable level of $100 trillion this would yield tax revenues of $200 billion for public purses. The same principle could be applied to stock exchanges, which would have the merit of stifling some of the endless churning of stocks in hedge funds which achieve little other than enriching traders and brokers.

Match risks and rewards

The most repulsive aspect of the 2008 financial crisis is that even disgraced chief executives of failed banks walked away with huge bonuses, as reward for failure. This is because the incentive systems encouraged employees to take bets on the markets that would produce short-term gains, in risky deals and crazy loans that would later turn toxic, by which time the trader or chief executive would have collected millions of dollars. This is akin to betting against a number coming up on a roulette wheel – you can take quite a few spins before being caught out, by which time you could have moved on to a different game. When chief executive Stan O'Neal was ousted from Merrill Lynch in October 2007 he was comforted with a $160 million pay-off, in part based on a rise in the share price that had yet to reflect his dangerous strategies. The pay for bankers and others should be based instead on continuous assessment of their performance, and where appropriate reflect the full implications of their activities even if these may not be known for several years. This will mean devising new contracts, so now is a good time while the bankers are looking for jobs and are not so picky about the perks.

Close tax havens

The world's tax havens serve no purpose other than to boost the profits of corporations and rich individuals at the expense of regular tax payers. The British government bears much of the responsibility since it is in a position to exert direct control over some of its own territories.[6] But there are other measures that could be taken to lift the veil of secrecy under which many companies and individuals operate, as they shuffle money from one dubious jurisdiction to another. This would involve, for example, demanding that companies declare the profits, losses, and taxes they pay in every country they do business. Just as important would be to end banking secrecy and to ensure that tax authorities in each country are able to exchange the necessary information.

A fresh start

The 2008 financial meltdown has had huge costs, not just for taxpayers in the rich countries but also for millions of people in developing countries who are suffering from a global economic crisis. But it also represents an opportunity for a fresh start – looking again at the most basic assumptions under which our financial systems operate.

The corporate lobbyists are, of course, busy preparing their arguments as to why it would be dangerous to react to the latest drama by stifling the creativity of financial markets. They claim that the latest crisis is simply part of a cycle of creative destruction, a Darwinian process that will permit the survival of the most robust financial models and sweep away those that have prove useless or dangerous.

But we now know the true cost of this free-for-all. The financial markets are not to be trusted. They expect to be given free rein to make huge profits while the sun is shining, but hasten to the shelter of the state when the skies darken. Never again. We now know better. Time to devise a new financial architecture.

1 Giles, C and S. de Daneshkhu, 2006. 'City of London offsets Budget tax shortfall', in *The Financial Times*, 26 March. 2 Ford, J. 2008. 'A greedy giant out of control', in *Prospect*, November. 3 *The Economist*, 2008. 'The end of the affair', in *The Economist*, 22 November. 4 Huber, J. and J Robertson, 2000. *Creating new money: A monetary reform for the information age*, London, New Economics Foundation. 5 Tricks, H. 2008. 'Dirty words', in The World in 2009, London, *The Economist*. 6 Mathiason, N and H Stewart, 2008. 'Obama backs crackdown on tax havens', in *The Observer*, 9 November.

Resources

Clean Start - www.newint.org/cleanstart/ New Internationalist campaign to build a fairer global economy.

Bretton Woods Project – www.brettonwoodsproject.org

Focus on the Global South – www.focusweb.org

The Transnational Institute – www.tni.org

Halifax Initiative Coalition – www.halifaxinitiative.org

Jubilee Debt Campaign – www.jubileedebtcampaign.org.uk

Third World Network – www.twnside.org.sg

The Corner House – www.thecornerhouse.org.uk

IFI Watch – www.ifiwatchnet.org

Eurodad – www.eurodad.org

Tax Justice Network – www.taxjustice.net

New Economics Foundation – www.neweconomics.org

James Robertson (green economist) – www.jamesrobertson.com

Microfinance Gateway – http://microfinancegateway.org/

Global Issues – www.globalissues.org

Money – past present and future – http://projects.exeter.ac.uk/RDavies/arian/money.html

World Council of Credit Unions – www.woccu.org

Grameen Bank – www.grameenbank.org

Bibliography

Money: A history, Catherine Eagleton and John Williams, British Museum Press, London, 2007.

Money: Whence It came, Where It Went. JK Galbraith, Houghton Mifflin Company, Boston.

The Origin of Financial Crises: Central banks, credit bubbles, and the efficient market fallacy. George Cooper, Harriman House, Petersfield 2008.

Guide to Financial Markets, Marc Levinson, Profile Books, London, 2006.

The Trillion Dollar Meltdown, Charles Morris, Public Affairs, New York, 2008.

An Introduction to Global Financial Markets, Stephen Valdez, Palgrave Macmillan. Basingstoke, 2007.

The Globalizers: the IMF, the World Bank, and their borrowers. Ngaire Woods 2006. Cornell University Press, Ithaca and London.

Unholy Trinity: the IMF, World Bank and WTO. Richard Peet, Zed Books, London and New York, 2003.

Stability with growth: Macroeconomics, liberalization and development, Joseph Stiglitz et al. Oxford University Press, New York.

Glossary

Asset – Something that provides its owner with some earning power. Banks, for example, consider the loans they make as their main assets.

Bond – A contract which set out the terms of a loan, stating what the payments, equivalent to interest, or 'coupon', will be, and when the loan must be repaid.

Capital – Wealth that can be used as a basis for creating more wealth. For a bank, the capital consists mostly of funds contributed by shareholders, plus accumulated profits. Banks need to have a minimum ratio of capital to loans, typically around 10 per cent, to serve as a buffer against bad loans or other losses.

Collateralized debt obligation (CDO) – A collection of bank loans that have been packaged up and then sold on in portions or 'tranches' to investors who are entitled to the income as loans are repaid.

Commercial paper – A type of short-term bond issued by companies.

Commodity money – Money whose value is set by the value of the material of which it is composed, anything from wheat to gold to cowrie shells.

Credit crunch – A sudden reduction in lending as banks become nervous about taking on almost any level of risk.

Credit default swap (CDS) – Insurance against default on a loan.

Derivatives – Financial assets that are based on, 'derived' from, other assets.

Dollarization – When a country replaces its own currency with the US dollar.

Fiat money – Money in the form of paper notes or coins whose value is backed by an authority, usually a government, which determines what is legal tender. The acid test is whether it is acceptable for payment of taxes.

Hedge fund – A fund which bets on changes in market prices using both investors' funds and borrowed funds.

Investment bank – Company that provides a range of advice and other financial services primarily to corporations or the very wealthy.

Leveraging – Magnifying the scale of an investment, and therefore the potential profits or losses, by using borrowed money.

Liquidity – Represents how easily an asset may be spent. Cash is fully liquid. Other assets such as shares or bonds are fairly liquid if they can easily be sold.

Money markets – Wholesale global markets, in which banks and other major institutions make large short-term loans of cash or other liquid assets such as government bonds.

Private equity company – A company which buys up all the shares of weak or undervalued public companies, rendering them 'private', then reorganizing the companies or breaking them up for profitable resale.

Quant – A fund that picks stocks in which to invest, primarily by using mathematical models.

Ratings agencies – Companies, such as Moody's, that rate the safety of bonds or other securities for investors. Ratings range from AAA at the top, to D for a company already in default.

Securitization – Converting anything, such as a bank loan, into an income-delivering security that can then be sold to another party.

Security – Any financial contract, such as a bond or share, which gives the owner a stake in an asset from which they can derive an income.

Short selling – Borrowing an asset, usually a share, selling it, and then hopefully buying it back later at a lower price, and thus earning a profit before giving it back to its owner.

Sovereign wealth fund – Fund owned by a government and used to make international investments.

Special purpose vehicle (SPV) – A company, often a trust, that is created to serve as an intermediary for a specific transaction, such as securitizing mortgages.

Sub-prime loan – A risky loan to a borrower in a weak financial position.

Vulture fund – A fund that specializes in buying 'distressed' loans from banks or companies that have given up on the chances of full repayment, and then sues the borrowers for every last dollar.

Index

Index

Index

Index